A Year of Free-Range Writing Celebrations
By Jenny Alexander

A Year of Free-Range Writing Celebrations is itself a celebration, bringing together articles from five years of Jenny Alexander's popular 'Free-Range Writing' column in Writing Magazine.

From 'Readers' Letters'

'Having experienced severe writer's block since the birth of my daughter, I decided I had nothing to lose by giving some of the *Free-Range Writing* exercises a try. At first the words trickled painfully, but then – the flow. An hour later I had two poems to share with my writing group, a plot for a short story, a piece of memoir which had given me personal insight and four article pitches – two of which were later commissioned by magazine editors. Not bad for an hour's free-ranging. I've vowed since to start every writing session like this and have been much more productive as a result.' Vicky Bourne, Kidderminster.

'Jenny Alexander's *Free-Range Writing* each month never fails to deliver inspiring prompts. I should confess its usefulness in my role as co-facilitator of a creative writing group. In the poetry section of Jenny's page in March, I was delighted to see her focus on tapping into our roots… Don't be surprised when this results in a batch of touching and memorable poetry.' Rosie Currie, Belfast

'I thoroughly enjoyed the free writing exercise in *Jolly Holiday*, particularly the seven-postcard challenge. The clear boundary of the number of postcards and the fact that you can't fit much writing on a postcard led me to focus my mind and my writing. A really enjoyable writing exercise.' Helen Widdowson, Harrogate

'The memoir exercise helped me reflect on my leap of faith into having a go at writing; ignoring the doubts, the critic – is it any good? – and simply writing for the pure unadulterated joy of putting pen to paper and letting my imagination fly.' Karen Rogers, Chard

'I particularly enjoyed the biscuit-themed *Free-Range Writing* exercise (*WM May*) and decided to use this as inspiration for my university assignment. Several drafts (and biscuit packets) later, not only did I pass my assignment, I also had so much fun writing it.' Sarah Whitfield Mullarkey, Warrington.

'What an inspiration Jenny Alexander is. As a new writer my two big obstacles are deciding what to write about and getting over that self-conscious thing about other people reading what you have written. Since starting Jenny's Free Range Wring exercises, I can't get away from the keyboard.' Rob Preece, Olney.

Published by Five Lanes Press
Copyright © 2023 Jenny Alexander
https://jennyalexander.co.uk/

The moral right of Jenny Alexander to be identified as the author of this work has been asserted.

All rights reserved. No part of this publication shall be reproduced, stored in or introduced into a retrieval system, or transmitted in any form or by any means (electronic, mechanical, photocopying, recording or otherwise) without the prior permission of the copyright owner.

Most of the free-range writing articles in this collection have been previously published in Writing Magazine.

Cover design by Rachel Lawston
Book design by Bek Pickard, Zebedee Design

ISBN paperback: 978-1-910300-32-9
ISBN eBook: 978-1-910300-31-2

ABOUT THE AUTHOR

Jenny Alexander has written scores of books for children and adults, both fiction and non-fiction. Her children's fiction includes Blue Peter Book Club choice, *How to Get What You Want, by Peony Pinker* and Red House Children's Book Awards Highly Commended, *Car-Mad Jack*. Her Young Adult novel, *Drift*, is recommended by Cruse Bereavement Care, and her children's non-fiction includes thirteen funny self-help books on topics such as bullying, happiness, resilience, kindness, stress, green living and effective learning.

Jenny Alexander's adult books on writing cover everything from inspiration to publication, and she has placed many articles in Mslexia, Writers' Forum, Writing Magazine and The Author. She runs writing courses and workshops both independently and for organisations such as The Society of Authors, The Scattered Authors' Society, Bridging Arts, Mantle Arts, Writing Magazine, The Arvon Foundation, The Writing Retreat and Lapidus ('Words for Wellbeing') as well as a wide variety of small independents such as writing groups, after school clubs and home-educating families.

A YEAR OF FREE-RANGE WRITING CELEBRATIONS

JENNY ALEXANDER

five lanes

CONTENTS

Introduction	13
January	15
Diving In	16
The Wisdom of Pooh	19
New Beginnings	22
World Snow Day	25
February	29
Storytelling Week	30
Book Giving	33
Black Monday	36
Random Acts of Kindness	40
March	43
Happiness	44
Old Stuff	47
Mother's Day	50
Make Your Day	53
April	57
April Fool's Day	58
Earth Day	60
Unicorns	63
Pets	66

May — 71

- Walking — 72
- Mental Health — 75
- Dying Matters — 78
- Biscuits — 81

June — 85

- Reading Groups — 86
- Father's Day — 89
- Knitting — 92
- Writing Day — 95

July — 99

- Friendship — 100
- Seaside — 103
- Plastic — 106
- Staycations — 109

August — 113

- Play — 114
- Owls — 117
- Holidays — 120
- Youth — 123

September — 127

- Swap Ideas Day — 128
- World Peace — 131
- Learning — 134
- Procrastination — 137

October	141
World Post Day	142
Older People	145
Libraries	148
Drawing	151
November	155
Bonfire Night	156
NaNoWriMo	159
Stress	162
Road Safety	165
December	169
Handmade Gifts	170
Elf Day	173
Volunteering	176
Christmas	179
Your Birthday Bonus	183
Happy birthday!	184
Tick list	187

INTRODUCTION

Every kind of personal writing is brilliant because knowing no one is going to read it gives you complete creative freedom to experiment and play.

When you free-range across different genres with your personal writing that introduces a whole new level of experimentation to delight your writer self, help you develop your writing voice and build your writing skills.

The free-range ideas in this book, being inspired by celebration days, also provide loads of new material by getting you thinking about topics you might never have given much thought to before.

Writing in this adventurous way is a gateway to living more adventurously too because when you are willing to go outside your comfort zone with your writing you gradually bring the same attitudes of 'Why not?' and 'Let's give it a go!' to the way you live your life.

And there's more.

Every kind of personal writing has been shown to boost well-being – it's a gift of time and attention that you give to yourself – and focusing on celebration days adds the extra positive benefit that well-being practices such as gratitude and mindfulness provide.

Although free-range writing is personal writing, you can use the ideas in this book to set up a monthly writing celebrations group, just sharing ideas and reading to each other if you want to at the end.

Whether you're writing on your own or in a group, the one rule is, stick to the timings. They're there to help you because your inner critic really hates to be hurried.

Note: These writing celebrations are arranged over a year, but you can start any time, either ignoring the actual month of writing and starting at New Year, or matching your writing celebrations to the month you are writing in. Or of course, you could just dive in and do them in any order you like – there's a tick list at the back to help you keep track of which ones you've done.

JANUARY

Diving In

The Polar Bear Plunge is a surprisingly popular New Year's Day tradition in many parts of the Northern Hemisphere, including the United Kingdom, the Netherlands, Canada and the USA, where people get together to jump into icy lakes and rivers, or run out into the wintry waves of the sea for charity.

Luckily, we writers don't have to actually strip off and dive in to get the cold-water swimming experience – we can do it in memory and imagination. Try it now – and then treat yourself to a nice cup of hot choc to warm up again!

Memoir

At my secondary school in the 1960's, we had an unheated outdoor pool, where compulsory swimming lessons took place every week throughout the summer term. It felt like a form of torture. Yet we happily hung out at Surbiton lagoon at weekends, where the water must have been just as cold though we never seemed to feel it.

What memories do you have of outdoor swimming or paddling in cold water? Write on this topic, just whatever comes, not worrying about chronological order, for five minutes.

It takes courage to step into the chilly waters around the UK. You have to take a deep breath, gear yourself up, make the decision and commit. You have to do the same thing every time you take the plunge metaphorically speaking too.

When you are tempted to dive into something new, do

you generally jump and worry later, worry and jump anyway or worry and step back? When did you take a plunge? When did you want to take a plunge, but didn't? Write for five minutes, just whatever comes.

Reading back over these two pieces of writing, decide which particular occasion you would like to write about. It could be either a literal swim or a metaphorical taking the plunge. Tell the story. Take about ten minutes.

Fiction

Someone decides to do the Polar Bear Plunge on New Year's Day because they want to raise money for a particular charity. They have never done it before, so why now? What is the charity? Where is the event taking place? Who helps and encourages them? Who doesn't? Jot down some ideas.

Do they succeed or fail? How do they feel about the outcome? In what way are they changed by the endeavour? Write the story, taking about twenty minutes.

> TIP: Who, what, where, why, when and how – asking these questions is the key to finding a story.

Non-Fiction

How much do you know about polar bears? This month's non-fiction foray is all about research, which is one of the pleasurable aspects of writing non-fiction. Learning new things triggers the same pleasure response in the brain as sex and drugs – there's science to prove it!

So find out some things you didn't know about polar bears, and make some notes. Did you know their skin is actually black and their fur is not white, for example?

Looking at your notes, think about what angle feels most interesting to you, and plan an article. Who is your target reader – adult or child? Which of the special features of non-fiction – for example, photos, maps, charts and graphs, fact boxes, sub-headings, bulleted or numbered lists – could you use to illustrate your points? Words are not the only way we convey information in non-fiction writing.

Take about twenty minutes to get the body of the article, making a note of where you would include photos, maps, charts and so on.

> TIP: Think visually when you write non-fiction, not just what the text will say but also how it will appear on the page.

Poetry

Imagine you are going for a winter swim in the sea, or perhaps a lake, a river or unheated outdoor pool. You are standing at the edge, gearing yourself up to go in. Close your eyes and use all your senses to picture the scene. Feel the chilly air on your skin and in your nostrils, as you draw a breath in. Feel the ground beneath your bare feet. How are you feeling emotionally? Where, in your body, are you experiencing those emotions? Take your time.

As you enter the water, notice all the sensations in your body. Notice your emotions, too. Are you feeling exhilarated? Panicky? How soon do you find your flow and how long do you stay in?

Write a poem about this experience of swimming in a cold, outdoor body of water. You will almost certainly be aware of symbolic resonances with this subject – situations in your life when you have felt those patterns of emotion – but don't make them explicit.

Make your poem a simple description of swimming in cold water, and let your reader find their own symbolic resonances. Take about twenty minutes.

The Wisdom of Pooh

Winnie the Pooh Day is in January, and what better way to start the year than with a dip into the wonderful wisdom of Pooh and his friends?

The great thing about personal writing is that no one else is going to read it, so it's a place you can experiment freely and play. You might find ideas that surprise you and decide to develop them further. Your free-range writing can be a seedbed of ideas for all your writing projects.

Memoir

Pooh says he gets to where he's going by walking away from where he has been. In your life, what have you walked away from in order to get to a new situation? What did you have to walk away from to get to where you are now?

Write for fifteen minutes, beginning 'I walked away from…' Repeat the prompt as many times as you like, whenever one idea ends and another one comes to mind.

Read back over what you have written. Feel how every new thing requires a letting go. What would you like more of in your life right now, and what you would you have to let go of in order to make space for it? Write for five minutes, just whatever comes.

Fiction

Pooh's friend, Christopher Robin, says that sometimes we are braver or cleverer than we think we are, and stronger than we seem.

In this story, someone is in a situation they do not believe they can handle. No one else expects them to handle it either. Jot down some ideas, using the usual questions: who, what, when, where and why?

Now think about the 'How?' How does this character triumph over the situation? What do they do that surprises both other people and themselves?

This story is an opportunity to think about show-don't-tell. How can you show what kind of person this is in normal life, without saying it directly? Supposing they are normally very shy, can you show they are shy in the way they behave or in how they are with other people at the beginning? When they do the surprising thing, how can you show that they and other people feel that it's out of character for them?

Stories have two plot strands – the action plot and the psychological journey. What has your main character learnt through this story? How are they changed by it? Take about fifteen minutes to write the story or, if you prefer, use the time to continue building your notes.

Non-Fiction

Philosophers have had fun with Pooh, finding in these simple stories instructions on how to live a good life based around simplicity, friendship, kindness and going with the flow. That is the tao, or way, of Pooh. What would be the tao of you?

In your view, what are the keys to living a happy life?

What should we nurture, and what should we avoid? Pooh nurtures pleasure and avoids striving; he loves his friends and lives close to nature. He is 'a bear of little brain' but he has a big heart.

Write a five- or ten-point plan for living a happy life. Take fifteen minutes. If you had to condense it down to one main idea, what would that be? Write a single sentence to summarise the most important thing.

Poetry

Pooh talks about the wisdom of rivers, which is that they know that there is no rush; whatever obstacles they meet, they will get where they are going in the end, because rivers always find their way to the sea.

Give your poem a title that begins, 'The Wisdom of…' and take its inspiration, as Pooh so often does, from nature. The wisdom of trees, or bees; of clouds or mountains or roses or sand, or indeed any natural phenomenon that you would like to explore. Go with your first idea.

Don't try to formulate the philosophical point before you start, but begin with the phenomenon itself, describing it in detail, its physical properties, and allowing any ideas that come to develop out of that. Take fifteen minutes.

Now play with your poem by making the thing you have chosen the narrator, giving their advice directly. You can find Ilan Shamir's famous poem online, 'Advice from a tree', if you need some inspiration. Or just find it anyway if you would like some wise advice! Take ten minutes.

New Beginnings

I love the turning of the year – it's the perfect time for beginnings. I like to start a new book in January, having spent the autumn laying the groundwork – that's been my pattern for many years. It reminds me of waiting for the wave on a body-board and catching it right at the start of its rush to the beach.

When it comes to my personal writing, I like to start a new notebook too, so January always feels like setting out on fresh journaling adventures. I recommend it!

Here are some free-range writing ideas for the turning of the year. Remember to stick to the timings – that way, you have to get stuck straight in, with no time for overthinking or procrastination.

Memoir

Think back over the last year and write some lists:

- three positive things that happened
- three negative things that happened
- three things that happened (or didn't happen!) in your writing life

Don't overthink it – just go with your first ideas, big or small.

After that, write about the last year, whatever comes, keeping your pen moving on the paper for ten minutes.

Reflect on what you've written. Notice what kind of thing you've chosen to focus on – your inner life and emotions, your day-to-day activities, places, people, relationships…? Write for another five minutes.

Fiction

Someone makes a New Year's resolution. Who? Write some character notes – their name, age, appearance. What is their resolution? Why is it important to them?

In early January, they are tempted to break their resolution – why? Where are they? Write some notes on the setting.

Someone else is involved, either in encouraging them to break their resolution or persuading them not to. What is their relationship with the protagonist, if any? Why do they try to intervene? What's the outcome?

Write the scene. Take twenty minutes.

> TIP: If you give your fictional protagonist one of your own New Year resolutions, the other character in this scene may show you either your inner strength of purpose or unconscious resistance in relation to it.

Non-Fiction

At the start of a new year, I set myself one big challenge, one small one and one inner challenge to the way I'm thinking. I like the idea of challenges rather than resolutions – it sounds more dynamic and less dogged.

What would you like to try and achieve in your writing life in the coming year? Think of some big things and some small ones and jot them down just as they occur to you – for example, 'Finish my novel', 'Write my diary every day', 'Go on a writing workshop', 'Enter a competition' or 'Tell my friends I've been secretly writing poetry for years.'

Only you know which of your writing challenges are big

or small. For some people, going on a workshop could be a fun thing they've just never got round to trying but, for others, it might feel like a terrifying step into the unknown.

Now think about your attitudes towards writing. What negative thoughts do you have that get in the way of your writing success and pleasure? 'I'm no good at it' – that's a common one. 'It's self-indulgent', 'Who would be interested in what I have to say?' Simply noticing when you're thinking those thoughts will help you let them go.

Choose one big challenge, one small one and one negative thought about your writing that you're intending to notice and let go.

Write a mission statement for your writing goals in the coming year. Email it to a friend if you feel that might help you stick to it.

Poetry

Imagine last year was a single day – what kind of weather would it be? Sunny, stormy, overcast and grey? What kind of place – countryside, beach, garden, office, kitchen, shopping mall?

Go with your first thoughts – there's no right or wrong decision in creative thinking. For example, the year I did a lot of writing workshops for organisations outside my local area could be a bright breezy day outside, with me in an unfamiliar hall or meeting room.

Close your eyes for a few minutes and use all your senses to fully imagine yourself in this setting. Notice how you feel emotionally, and where you feel those emotions in your body.

Write a poem simply describing this place, in this day of weather, and what it feels like to be there. See if any thoughts or insights about where you've been and where you would like to be, going forward, start to emerge through that. Take twenty minutes.

World Snow Day

World Snow Day falls in January, which is the most likely time of year for us in the UK to see some snow. The idea is to raise interest in snow sports such as skiing and snowboarding and encourage children and their families to create lasting memories of the wonders of snow. Hopefully, there will be some real-life inspiration outside your window when you do your free-range writing, but even if it's mild and muggy you can still enjoy finding snowy inspiration in your memories and imaginings.

Keep your free-range writing across the genres brisk and breezy by sticking to the timings.

Memoir

Christmas night, London in the sixties, standing in the middle of our road with my sisters and brother and our cousin; snow up to the tops of our wellies and deep holes for footprints from the front door to here. Absolute silence. Cars half buried, street lights making pools of brighter white on white...

Sledging with my kids on holidays in Scotland. Midwinter on the ferry North from Tromso, just me, hearing the tinkle of surface ice against the side of the ship as it moves through the water between snow-covered islands.

Jot down some snowy memories of your own, from any stage in your past. Choose one. Close your eyes and fully remember it, using all your senses, the feel of the air on your skin and in your nostrils, the quality of the light, the sounds. What were you wearing? Notice how your body feels inside your clothes, and your feet inside your shoes.

Take about five minutes remembering and making notes. If you haven't had many snowy experiences yourself, what snowy stories have you heard from family members and friends? You could ask them for more details, or fill in the details yourself, from imagination. Memoir writing, like memory itself, is a variable mix of objective facts and imagination.

Choose one memory and take fifteen minutes to tell the story.

Fiction

Snow isn't always fun, and in this story, someone is cut off by snow and it's a particular problem for them… why?

Someone else realises they are in trouble and helps them… how?

Make some notes on the characters, circumstances and settings. Decide which character interests you more, the one that needs help or the rescuer. Make that one your main character, telling the story in either the first person, 'I', as them, or the third person, 'he/she' from their point of view.

With this story, there's a particular opportunity for pathetic fallacy, or expressing the mood of the main character in the way you describe the settings. Are they lost in the hills and afraid of freezing to death? Your snow could be driven in on a biting wind, it could be a white-out. Are they stranded in their car and afraid of being buried? This snow could be blanketing, enveloping, falling heavily.

Are they feeling low? The pavements could be slushy and slippery, and the white flecks of snow floating in a dark grey sky.

Tell the story. Take twenty minutes.

Non-Fiction

There's a good reason why numbered list articles are so popular – they are quick and easy to read, and they are also easy to write and research. Search facts about snow online. You'll find plenty, so your job is to choose the best ones, the ones that go together. Selecting material from research is a key non-fiction writing skill.

For example, if you've been outside in the snow, you may have noticed that it muffles sound, but did you know that when it melts and then refreezes, ice magnifies sound? How many kinds of snowflake are there? Can a single snowflake measure more than a foot across?

Choose five to ten fascinating facts and write an article, beginning with a sentence of introduction before your numbered list. Add a sentence of summary at the end. Take twenty minutes in total.

Poetry

Once upon a time, before the world froze over…

Imagine a future world where climate change has brought a new ice age. In this poem, you are writing as an elder, describing for a young person who has never known anything different, what the world was like before everything was covered in snow. Your poem will have a mythic quality, describing landscapes, animals, plants and a way of living that your young reader can only imagine.

Or if you prefer, your post-apocalyptic world could be

a scorched desert, where younger people have never experienced cold days in nature or seen snow, and now never will. Snow in this world is the stuff of legend; it exists only in the stories the elders tell.

Fully imagine your world, but when you come to write the poem, remember it's a poem about snow. Snow is your focus, so give your poem a title that reflects that. Take twenty minutes.

FEBRUARY

Storytelling Week

National Storytelling Week runs from the last days of January into the beginning of February, and it's a time when storytellers perform throughout the UK in clubs, theatres, museums, schools, hospitals and care homes.

Everyone loves a good story. We tell stories to ourselves all the time – it's our nature. We make decisions by imagining different future scenarios and understand the past by organising our experiences into the stories of memory. Even when we are asleep, our minds are continuously creating stories in our dreams.

So, relax and do what comes naturally, exploring different ways to tell stories in memoir, fiction, non-fiction and poetry.

Memoir

When did you make a life-changing decision? For example, moving to a new home, starting or ending a relationship, having a baby, taking a new job or giving up an old one.

What was the outcome? Tell the story. Five minutes.

If you hadn't made that decision, what might you have done instead? Imagine how things might have turned out differently. Write just whatever comes into your head, exploring that for about five minutes.

Notice how your 'would have' and 'could have' thoughts are all stories.

Now write down five things that are on your bucket list – that is to say, things you'd like to do before you kick it.

Choose one. What would it be like if you did it? It could be amazing – write the story! It could be disappointing or even catastrophic. Write that story too. Take a few minutes for each version.

Fiction

Imagine a stranger tells you a story about something that has happened to them. It might be a person sitting beside you on a train, for example, or a shopkeeper having a bad day, or a fellow dog-walker on a towpath.

Write some notes about this character – their age, appearance and body language.

Where does this encounter take place? Close your eyes and picture the scene. Hear their voice as they tell their story.

Now imagine you are the person telling the story. What does it feel like to be in that body, in those clothes and shoes? What are you feeling emotionally, and what are the physical effects of those emotions?

In the first person, 'I', tell their story. Take fifteen minutes.

Non-Fiction

Narrative non-fiction is a kind of creative or literary non-fiction that follows a story-like shape and uses the techniques of fiction. It has to be factually accurate but also carry the reader along in the same way as fictional stories do. Memoirs and biographies are narrative non-fiction, and so is a lot of travel writing.

Jot down some places you have visited or been to on holiday. Choose one and make some notes on the story elements of your visit.

- When and why did you go? What did you want or expect from the visit? Plot almost always comes from what the main character wants.

- The settings – not just what the place itself was like but also the season, the weather and the time of day.
- The action. What happened to either satisfy or thwart your expectations? Maybe you didn't just see the otters but got to feed them; maybe the meal was lacking in flavour and overpriced. Think of several things that made your experience of the place what it was for you.
- The outcome. What is your conclusion from your visit? What did you learn?

Write the true story. Fifteen minutes.

Poetry

Like narrative non-fiction, narrative poetry uses the elements of fiction to tell a story. It needs characters and action (something has to happen), with a compelling opening and a satisfying ending.

In this poem, someone receives some great news. For example, it could be their doctor giving them the all clear or their driving examiner telling them they've passed the test. Think of a few scenarios and choose one.

Write some notes about the character – just their name, age and something about their appearance. Picture the scene where they receive this great news. Who gives them the good news? Where does it happen? More notes.

Tell the story of this meeting in a poem. Keep it free verse unless your intention is humorous, in which case a regular pattern of rhyme and rhythm can boost the comic effect. Take about fifteen minutes. If you like the poem and it isn't quite right yet, continue playing with the words and ideas for as long as it takes.

> TIP: Poetry doesn't have to follow any set pattern of rhythm and rhyme. What makes it different from prose is partly that it looks like a poem on the page, with lots of white space around it. The poet Philip Gross says that white space is room for the reader to bring their own thoughts and feelings in. I love that! Because a poem is so short, you can enjoy playing with the language until every word sounds right.

Book Giving

Last year, in a city park, I came across a children's book, with a tag that said, 'Whoever you are, this is for you. Happy Book Giving Day!' I counted six children's books in the park that day.

International Book Giving Day takes place on 14th February, the aim being to get books into the hands of as many children as possible and promote a love of reading in the young.

Check out their website if you would like to take part, but in the meantime, celebrate your love of books with these Book Giving Day free-range ideas. Stick to the timings – your inner critic really does hate to be rushed.

Memoir

When did you discover the joy of reading? I hardly possessed a single book as a child, but I got into reading in my late teens when I discovered second-hand book shops. I only realised all the great children's books I had missed out on when I got my first job, in Prestwick branch library, and then I read every children's book on the shelves.

What particular books have helped or entertained you at different periods in your life? Do you have favourite kinds of book for different circumstances, such as on holiday or on the bus to work?

Starting as far back as you remember, write the story of reading in your life. Take twenty minutes.

If you would like to encourage the joy of reading in a child, choose a book and leave it somewhere it can be found. Then, for a bonus bit of memoir, write for ten minutes on why you chose that particular book, where you left it and what kind of child you hope will pick it up.

Fiction

Stories have two plotlines – the action plot and the psychological plot – and you can start building your ideas from either. In the psychological plot, the protagonist is unsettled by a negative emotion – maybe they feel jealous or unhappy or unfulfilled – and the action of the story brings them to some kind of psychological resolution – at the very least, they come to terms, or learn a valuable lesson.

So, for this story, start with the psychological situation of the protagonist, and imagine a child who feels angry, anxious or sad. Picture them in your mind or search online and choose a photo you can relate to. Write some character notes – their name, age, physical appearance, some things they care about, some things they dislike.

Why is this child feeling emotionally unsettled, and how unsettled are they? It could be a very minor upset or a major struggle that they're going through.

In your story, the child finds a book on Book Giving Day. Where? Who else, if anyone, is there? What is the book? You don't need to know any real children's books – you can conjure one up in imagination, give it a title and an author, picture the cover.

At the end of the story, the child feels a little better, or maybe a lot. They gain some kind of insight or inspiration. It's as simple as that! Write the story for twenty minutes.

Non-Fiction

A third of children in the UK today do not possess a single book; in the US, that figure is higher. These children are missing out on much more than a hobby, because a love of reading at a young age is linked to higher achievement across the school curriculum.

Dolly Parton is a champion of children's reading, and her Imagination Library has sent over 100 million books to children in thousands of communities across the USA, Canada, UK, Australia and Ireland.

What was her inspiration for this amazing project? How does it work? Do some research. Jot down some notes.

Tell the story in one sentence.

Tell it again in half a page.

And again, in a whole page.

Take as long as it takes – research can lead you down interesting pathways!

> TIP: Being able to adjust the length by adding or cutting is an essential skill in all forms of writing. It is often a big part of the work of redrafting – if you write lean in the first instance, like I do, redrafting means putting flesh on the bones; if you write long, the job will often involve paring it down.

Poetry

Every book is a gift from the writer to the reader – that's why I personally do not post bad reviews, it would feel rude and unkind, like criticising a birthday present.

Imagine you have written a children's book. Feel the heft of it in your hands; see the style and colours of the cover image, the title and your author name. Picture your reader. What do you hope your book will give them?

What message or dedication would you like to include at the front? Write it in the form of a rhyming poem – children like their poems to rhyme. Take ten minutes.

Black Monday

The first Monday in February is the day when UK workers are most likely to call in sick and, although the commonest excuses are colds, flu and food poisoning, most people who opt for staying under the duvet on 'black Monday' admit the real reason is because they just don't feel like getting up.

Lethargy and gloom can set in around this time, with cold dark months behind us and weeks still to go before the arrival of spring, but there is warmth and pleasure to be found in the depths of winter too, and this month's free-range writing is all about finding it.

Pleasure is the point of personal writing. If you enjoy doing something, you want to do it more, and the more you do it the better you get at it. So rather than starting from theory and technique, I encourage people to find and develop their writing voice through writing. One rule: stick to the timings!

Memoir

In nature, many animals become dormant or hibernate through the winter, and many plants die right back before bursting with new growth in the spring. We humans need periods of quiet inertia too, when we may feel directionless or becalmed, while beneath the surface energy is building for new beginnings.

Sometimes we might deliberately take time out with a holiday or career break, but quite often, these fallow times feel unwelcome, brought about by physical illness, for example, or grief or depression. Some writers think of these inactive periods as 'writer's block,' rather than a natural part of the creative process.

When has your life, or an area of your life such as your writing or relationship, felt becalmed? Jot down some ideas and choose one. What was your life like just before everything ground to a halt? And what happened afterwards, what new beginning, when you came out of it?

Write for twenty minutes, whatever comes. As one idea runs out, move on to another one.

Fiction

'Pathetic fallacy' is when a writer uses the setting to reflect and amplify the emotion of a scene. Is trouble brewing? Cue storm clouds. Is romance in the air? Cue balmy nights and moonlight. Is the pursuer closing in? Darkness, thunder, crack of lightning!

This month's fiction is all about exploring the power of pathetic fallacy by picturing a character in the depths of gloom and lethargy on 'black Monday' and describing the setting in a way that reflects their mood or situation. You don't need to tell the whole story – the task is just to conjure this psychological moment and a setting that amplifies the emotion of it.

Imagine this moment as an atmospheric photo. Here is somebody who feel completely incapable of facing the day. Maybe they're still in bed, after a sleepless night, or gazing out the window as the morning hours tick by, or sitting on their back step, smoking a cigarette. Picture every detail in this photo, the objects in the background, the colours and tones; look closely at the character, their facial expression, their body language, what they are wearing.

Describe exactly what you see in the photo, taking about ten minutes. Then read back over your description and see if there are any other ways you might use the setting to intensify your character's 'black Monday' feelings. Write a second draft. Take ten minutes.

Non-Fiction

For this non-fiction piece, imagine you are the editor of a magazine – it could be one that already exists or one you make up, on a theme that interests you, such as crafting or fishing or family life.

What is the magazine called? Picture the cover.

You have been sent a choice of articles for your February edition including how-to's, personal stories, numbered lists and interviews with experts… Jot down some ideas.

Select two or three of the article pitches that you think might help and encourage your readers to get through the dark days of February.

Now write your editorial. For inspiration, check out some back issues of your favourite magazine, and see how the editor introduces the theme for each edition. That's the kind of length you're looking for. Take up to twenty minutes.

Poetry

Everyone has gloomy days in the dark time of the year so start from your own experience with a prose warm-up, writing whatever comes about occasions when it was cold and dark outside, and you felt fed up and lethargic.

How did you get through? What helped? Did you bunk off work, or go on a long walk, or message a friend? I do all those when I'm feeling slightly down – if it's really bad, I resort to household chores, reckoning that as I'm not going to enjoy the day anyway, I might as well at least have something to show for it.

Write, keeping the pen moving on the paper, for ten minutes, just whatever comes.

Choose one occasion for your poem. Capture the feeling of the season through the physicality of the experience, the chill in the air, the low winter light. How did you feel emotionally at the time, and how do you feel now, looking back? Take twenty minutes.

> **TIP**: Writing a poem is like dropping a pebble in a pond, it's a small thing that sets up lots of resonances. Reading back over your poem, does it give you any insights into how you handle difficult times generally in life?

Random Acts of Kindness

February 17th is Random Acts of Kindness Day. It's about actions, not just good intentions, and these actions might be random because they come from someone you don't know or random because they come unexpectedly and for no particular reason from someone you do.

When I drafted this article, I made a note in the margin to think of a real-life example, before stopping for lunch. I'd barely sat down with my sandwich when some flowers arrived from my daughter with a note that said, 'Just because...' Job done!

Kindness usually feels good, both to the giver and the receiver, and that makes it a really pleasurable theme to explore in free-range writing. Enjoy – and remember, stick to the timings, because then you don't have time to sit staring at a blank sheet of paper and your inner critic can't get a look in.

Memoir

Jot down a few ideas for the following, just whatever comes:

- When did someone you didn't know do or say something that helped?
- When did someone you know well do or say something surprising that helped?
- When did you do something to help a stranger?
- When did you do something surprising to help someone you know?

Write the story of one of them – fifteen minutes.

Fiction

The inspirational poet and writer, Khalil Gibran, said that kindness was not a sign of weakness but of strength. Sometimes it can be easier to walk by on the other side of the road, telling yourself you would do something if, if, if…

In this story, someone needs the kindness of strangers – who? What's the problem? Where are they? What's the weather like? What time of day is it? Write some notes.

Who helps? What do they say or do?

This random act of kindness has a knock-on effect for both of them – what is it?

Decide whose point of view feels more interesting to you and tell the story of their encounter in the first person, 'I…' Take twenty minutes.

Non-Fiction

Stream of consciousness writing – just scribbling down whatever comes, without planning or pausing – can be a great way of developing your ideas. Write for 5 minutes each in response to these kindness questions:

- Why is it important to be kind to yourself?
- Why is it important to be kind to the people you know?
- Why is it important to be kind to strangers?

Then explore the subject from a different angle and write for 5 minutes about unkindness. Notice how you feel when you flip it in this way.

> TIP: Emotion is great fuel for writing. Love, joy, anger, fear... noticing how you feel when you're writing will help you to harness that power.

Poetry

Sometimes you have to be cruel to be kind, because kindness is selfless – it looks to the best interests of the other, rather than our own comfort and convenience. Many pet owners have experienced this, when a cat or dog, for example, is terminally ill and the kindest thing is to ask the vet to end their suffering.

Every parent has experienced it, when they have to take a step back and let their child make mistakes or watch their frustration as they try and try to do something it would be very easy to do for them. There's wonderful poem about this called 'For Julia, in the Deep Water', by John N Morris – you can find it online.

Your poem will be the story of someone who has to do something cruel to be kind. What do they have to do? Why is it the kindest thing? Write some notes about the person and their dilemma.

Imagine you are this character and take five minutes to write the story in prose – just as it comes, in the first person, 'I...' Using prose warm-ups like this for writing poetry can help you feel your way into the voice of the poem.

Take fifteen minutes to write your poem, choosing either first person as in your warm-up or third person, 'he/she...'

> TIP: We tend to assume the 'I' in a poem represents the poet him- or herself. It is not necessarily so!

MARCH

Happiness

Experimenting with different genres is a great way of extending your range and developing your writing voice. For example, I started writing poetry because I wanted to be able to write more lyrical prose.

It can surprise you too. If you think of yourself as purely a fiction writer you might discover, when you free-range off your normal writing tracks, that you love writing non-fiction and poetry just as much. It's all about growing your writing happiness.

The International Day of Happiness falls in March, so with these writing forays that's both the practice and the theme. Happy writing!

Memoir

Some people who come to memoir writing workshops begin by saying they have only happy memories of childhood, others only sad. Writing is a way of remembering more fully, of rediscovering bright moments in dark places and dark ones on the sunny uplands of the past.

When did you feel happy? Jot down some memories from different stages of your life – your early childhood, secondary school years, young adulthood and so on, up through the decades to where you are now. These don't have to be big occasions – some of my most intensely happy moments have been when nothing out of the ordinary was happening at all.

Choose one memory to write about and tell the story. Take about twenty minutes. Really feel those happy emotions. Writing memoir can be an opportunity to enjoy wonderful experiences all over again.

> TIP: Emotions are experienced in the body: they are not abstract ideas. So the key to remembering how you felt more vividly and conveying it to readers is to focus on the physical symptoms of emotion rather than looking for abstract words to describe it. My heart raced… his eyes lit up…

Fiction

Happiness is a good theme for fiction because the protagonist always has a problem, that is to say, something he or she isn't happy about. That's the grit in the oyster, from which the story grows. No problem, no story.

The main plotline has two strands, first the action and second the psychological journey of the protagonist who, through the action, reaches a point of either triumph and breakthrough, or coming to terms – both of which are kinds of happiness. This means you can start imagining a story in either of two ways, with a situation or an emotion.

Start this story with someone who is suffering from an uncomfortable emotion – for example, anger, jealousy, sadness or fear. Who? Write some notes including, at the very least, their name, age and something about their appearance, but ideally explore a bit further into their current circumstances and key experiences in the past. The better you know your protagonist, the easier it is to write their story.

Why are they feeling the way they do? What has happened to trigger that emotion?

They do something that makes them feel better. What?

Take about twenty minutes to write the story.

Non-Fiction

There is a whole science of happiness now. Academics and therapists are looking beyond mood-altering drugs and psychological therapies to try and discover practical lifestyle choices that can help people feel happier.

For some time, doctors have been prescribing exercise and getting out into nature instead of antidepressants, and personal writing has recently been recognised as having similar benefits.

Search 'is writing good for your mental health?' or some such question and follow the leads that interest you, jotting down any interesting facts you find. For example, did you know research shows that writing is beneficial for your physical health as well as your mental wellbeing?

Research is one of the pleasurable elements of writing non-fiction and pleasure is a great wellbeing booster, so take your time and enjoy it. Then write a brief personal reflection on how you found the experience of researching this topic, including anything you discovered that surprised you. Take five minutes for the writing.

Poetry

'The blue bird of happiness' – that's a common metaphor. In my memoir section here, I used 'the sunny uplands.'

Find your own symbols for happiness by jotting down the first thoughts that come into your head, not censoring your ideas or overthinking, for an animal you associate with happiness, then a colour, a kind of weather, a kind of music and a place.

Write about each one for three minutes, whatever comes,

simply describing them without trying to link them to the theme of happiness at all.

Choose one of your prose pieces to develop into a poem. Don't spell out that your subject is a symbol for happiness, just enjoy the happy feelings that writing about it gives you and let the reader join the dots. Take ten minutes.

Old Stuff

In springtime, people often think about redecorating and extending their living spaces, or at least having a good clear out, so it isn't surprising that Old Stuff Day falls at the beginning of March. Old Stuff Day doesn't necessarily mean getting rid of things you don't need any more – it's a day for noticing your old stuff and deciding what you want to do with it. Some things you might want to cherish forever, but others you probably won't.

You can stick to the physical objects in your home or extend the idea to notice the things you have been doing the same way for years. Have you had the same hairstyle forever – could you maybe try a new one? Do you walk the same route with your dog every day?

Free-range writing is a practice designed to help you shake things up and not get stuck in a writing rut. Do you always write poems? Try a magazine article – you might enjoy it! And thinking like a non-fiction writer might give you new ideas you could bring back to your poetry writing too. There's only one rule: stick to the timings.

Memoir

There's a fascinating series called 'A History of the World in 100 Objects' on BBC Radio 4 in conjunction with the British Museum, where the presenter chooses artifacts from different times and places that give a flavour of what life was like when they were created.

Dividing your life into five periods, choose a single object from each one that you feel expresses the person you were at that time, and says something about your social situation. Title your piece, 'The story of my life in five objects' and write a sentence of introduction. Then, using the objects as subtitles, write a paragraph about each one. Start by describing it and go on to explain what it says about you and your life during that period.

Take twenty minutes.

> TIP: Go with the first objects that come into your head, however random they may feel. Trust your instincts. Surprise yourself!

Fiction

Someone has thrown away something they once valued very much – who, what, why? Did they throw it away deliberately, for example in anger or grief? Or was it an accident? Now they want or need to get it back.

Why do they need it – has something changed? How can they go about getting it back? Is there someone who could help? Is there someone who might try to stop them? Jot down some ideas.

Write the story, from when they lose this object to when

they find it again – or fail to find it. By the end, what have they learnt from the experience? Take twenty minutes.

Non-Fiction

Decluttering is on trend – bestselling books have been written about it, whole careers launched and developed. I'm definitely not a declutterer myself, but I do like to keep a flow, either moving things I've stopped really noticing to different places in my house or giving them away.

Most people have old things in their house they no longer really notice or need – what would your advice be for deciding what should go? Have you got any tips on how to store, display and look after the old stuff you decide to keep?

Write an opinion piece on organising your stuff. It does not have to represent your actual opinions – you can make it humorous and tongue-in-cheek if you like.

Back up your opinions with examples – these can be genuine or made up to illustrate your points. 'My great aunt could never throw a newspaper away and...' leading to whatever dire consequences or unexpected benefits will prove your point.

Take twenty minutes.

Poetry

Of course, old stuff may not be without value or charm. A lot of people are collectors of vintage toys, coins, stamps, board games – all sorts of things. This poem will be about a collector.

Who? Picture the character and write some notes – their name, age, something about their appearance. What do they collect? How long have they been doing it? How did it start?

Where do they look for more items for their collection? Do they also sell? Do they know other collectors socially? How do they feel about collecting – do they view it as a passion, an amusement, a job... an addiction?

Close your eyes and imagine you are this character. Adopt their body language – how does it feel to be a little stooped or breathless, skinny, stocky, old and tired or full of the energy of youth? Look at your collection – weigh some of the objects in your hands. Notice how you feel emotionally.

Now writing in the first person, as this character, write a poem describing your collection and what you love about collecting. Or, if you prefer, you could focus your poem on one or two objects from your collection. Either way, begin, 'It is...'

Take twenty minutes.

Mother's Day

Mother's Day, or Mothering Sunday, falls in March, and mothering is a rich theme to explore in writing. Mothering doesn't only come from our personal mothers, but all the women who have helped and nurtured us, such as grandmothers or aunts, teachers, sisters, friends. We refer to our mother country, mother nature, mother earth – the places we come from and return to, that give us a sense of belonging.

Nurture your creativity with some mothering-themed free-range writing. Give it unconditional love by keeping the inner critic away. To help with that, stick to the timings.

Memoir

I was not close to my mother or my grandmothers or aunts, but I have been blessed with some wonderful mothering, first from my older sister, Susan, then my tutor, Jean, several warm women friends and always from mother nature in the wild places I have lived.

Think about the mothering you have received in your life. Who has been home for you, your place of safety? Write whatever comes, about all your mother-figures, for fifteen minutes. Then take five minutes to write, in letter form, to one of the people you have described, starting, 'Dear…'

When you have written your letter, consider where you feel nurtured generally in your life. Writing is nurturing for me; it gives me a feeling of coming home to myself. For others, it might be sport or religion, the 'mother church', or gardening, where they say you are closest to God. Write for five minutes.

Fiction

Someone is in need of mothering. Who? Write some notes – their name, age and something about their appearance. What do they think is important? What do they not value at all? What are their circumstances? Where do they live, and who with? You won't use everything you know about your characters, but the better you know them, the easier it will be to know how they will react in the situation of the story. Write some notes.

Why does this character need some nurturing right now? Who offers them the nurturing they need? Build a sense of this second character in the same way as the first one, looking at their circumstances and values as well as their appearance. More notes.

What is the relationship between these two? How long have they known each other? What brings them together for the action of this story?

How is the first character's situation changed, at the end of the story, because of this second person, and the nurturing they give? What is possible for them now, that wasn't possible before? How is the relationship between these two changed, because of the story?

Write the story. Take twenty minutes.

Non-Fiction

A lot of people don't like Mother's Day because they see it as nothing more than a commercial opportunity, and it certainly is that. Cafes and restaurants, stately homes and gardens, even businesses such as steam railways and animal parks, can get in on the Mother's Day market.

Where do people go for days out in your area? List between three and five local venues. What might those places do for a special Mother's Day promotion? I remember one year at the Birsay tearooms in Orkney, they had a display table with Mother's Day muffins, each beautifully wrapped and presented, just inside the door, like goody bags for mothers. Some restaurants do 'mums eat free' promotions, or a complementary dessert or glass of wine.

When you have an idea for a promotion for each of your local venues, write a numbered article called something like, 'Five great ways to celebrate Mother's Day in... (your local town or county)' Start each section with a few sentences describing the venue and then the Mother's Day promotion they are offering. Writing non-fiction is an opportunity to think creatively and spark up new ideas. Take twenty minutes.

Poetry

We come from our mothers, whether we knew them or not, whatever kind of relationship we had or have with them, and your poem this month is about where you come from. For inspiration, search online for Robert Seatter's wonderful poem, 'I come from.'

Seatter describes the suburban environment of his childhood, giving us details of his family life that build to a strong sense of their values and anchor him in a particular moment in time, when children had clean handkerchiefs and read I-Spy Observer books.

Start your poem with the geographical setting of your childhood home and build a picture of your family life from details, as Seatter does. Use the prompt, 'I come from' as often as you like. Think about the movement and shape of your poem. Can the ending echo the beginning in some way, as Seatter's does, starting and closing with the trains?

Take twenty minutes.

Make Your Day

Today is National Stay in Bed and Read a Book Day. Not really – I made it up!

There are lots of great official celebration days in March but, to celebrate the springtime of year, I'm going to suggest you nominate your own brand-new unofficial day.

You know the rule by now: stick to the timings. Dive

straight in and don't give your inner critic a chance to get in the way.

Memoir

Like memoir writing, choosing your own celebration day is all about you. To get in the zone, start by writing some lists

- Activities you love doing – for example, walking, watching TV, sitting in cafes.
- Places you love – for example, Scotland, my garden, Trafalgar Square.
- People you enjoy seeing – for example, my brother, my writing group, my friend Angie.

Choose two things, from separate lists. For example, walking and Angie, or watching TV and Scotland. Create an unofficial celebration day from those – 'National Walk with a Friend Day', 'Watch a Film Set in Scotland Day.'

Imagine the website for your unofficial celebration day – what would the colour scheme be? The pictures? Describe the home page – take two or three minutes.

This website has a page for people's personal stories. What personal story could you contribute? Write about one or more occasions in your life when you have celebrated your unofficial national day. Take ten minutes.

Imagine how you might celebrate it next time. Fully imagine it. Notice how you feel emotionally, and where you experience those emotions in your body. Experiencing something in imagination can be as powerful as in real life, so really enjoy it. Then, write about the experience for five minutes.

Fiction

Create three more unofficial celebration days from your lists in the memoir task. Choose one.

For this story, imagine someone is celebrating the day you have chosen. Who?

Write some character notes, including their name, age and appearance. Start getting a feel for who they are by thinking of something that gives them pleasure and something that annoys or upsets them. If anyone else is involved, write some brief notes about them too.

Why does this character need a celebration day right now? That's the set-up.

What happens when they celebrate it? That's the action.

In what way does it make them feel better – or worse? That's the ending.

Tell the story. Twenty minutes.

Non-Fiction

Choose one of the unofficial celebration days you created for your memoir and fiction tasks. Imagine it has become an official thing, recognised either nationally or internationally. Write a few sentences of introduction and then set the rest of your article out in a question-and-answer form, asking the questions you think your imaginary readers will be interested in.

For example, who invented this celebration day? Answer, you! Name and describe yourself.

When did they invent it, and why? A bit of history here.

Where is it celebrated and by whom? Maybe your celebration day is celebrated in cities or villages, on beaches or in offices. Maybe it is particularly enjoyed by families, or teachers, or older people.

How can people celebrate it? Here, give some tips and suggestions.

Finish by summing up your answers in a sentence and making your own observations about this celebration day.

Take twenty minutes.

Poetry

Supposing greetings cards shops sold cards for one of the special celebration days you have created. Imagine them in a display. What kind of images might they have on the front? Would there be a colour scheme that runs through them? Could some of them be funny and some serious?

In imagination, pick one out. What is the greeting on the front? For example, 'Happy Stay in Bed and Read a Book Day…'

For this month's poetry task, write a little poem to go inside your card. Experiment with different versions – one of the great things about writing a poem is that it's easy to move things around. Try some rhyming versions and some non-rhyming.

Pick a few different cards from your display and write some little poems for those as well. Take a total of about twenty minutes.

> TIP: People say, 'Write about what you know', and it is easy to overlook what's familiar to us because we may not realise it will be new and interesting to other people. I would add, 'Write about what you love.' Love is the energy that fuels creativity. The great psychologist, Carl Jung, describes it perfectly when he says that 'the creative mind plays with the objects it loves.'

APRIL

April Fool's Day

In the tarot, the archetypal Fool takes a leap into the unknown, full of the joys of spring, not knowing or caring what lies ahead, and that is the spirit of April Fool's Day.

It's also a part of the writing process because no matter how much we plan, we never know exactly how it will turn out.

Take a joyful leap into the unknown now with these free-range writing forays.

Memoir
When did you take a leap of faith? Try to think of occasions from different stages of your life and include some major examples and some minor ones. Five minutes.

Choose one.

What did you do? How did it feel – before and after? What did you want to happen? What did happen? What could have gone wrong?

Write for fifteen minutes.

Fiction
Write a list of new ventures that start with a leap of faith. Include a few big ones, such as a first date, a new job, a new home, and a few smaller ones, such as trying a new restaurant, starting a course or pressing 'send'.

Choose one.

Someone is taking this leap – who? Picture the person.

Jot down some notes about your character – how old are they? Name? Appearance? Get a sense of their personality – what do they love? What do they hate? And a sense of their history – what's their earliest memory? Who would they try to avoid on the street? Who has been on their side? Take 5 minutes.

What made them decide to take the leap? How long had they been thinking about it?

Start writing the story, keeping it open in your mind whether it will all end in triumph or tears. Be like the April Fool and just set out, not knowing how the story will end.

Write for fifteen minutes.

Non-Fiction

When I was a girl, there used to be a song on the radio about fools rushing in where wise men never go... but on the other hand, the song said, wise men never fall in love, so what would they know about anything?

The Fool has his own kind of wisdom. He's an optimist. He may not see the pitfalls of moving forward, but he can see the possible benefits.

Write a non-fiction piece called, 'Five benefits of being an optimist.' The numbered list is a common format for blog posts and magazine articles, and it's very easy to write.

Start with a few sentences to introduce your subject. For example, you could check out my introductory section at the top of this article.

Then write a list of benefits, with a sentence or two about each one. (If you've only got three or four, or if you don't want to stop at five because you've got so many, just change the number in the title).

Round it off with a sentence of conclusion, summing up the benefits of being optimistic.

> TIP: If you're a dyed in the wool pessimist, you might find this one challenging. But look on the bright side – that means it'll be an even better mental workout for you!

Poetry

Listen to Lady Gaga sing *The Edge*. Feel how the lift in the lyrics seems to push higher and higher towards a leap.

What do you want to do that you haven't had the courage to commit to? What might happen if you did it – your hopes and fears?

Close your eyes and take a deep breath. You've been thinking about it for ages, and you're about to take the plunge.

How do you feel? Where do you feel these emotions in your body?

Write a poem in the first person. Don't try to make it fit any rhyme pattern or regular rhythm. This is not the moment for constraints! Keep it free, feel the feelings. Twenty minutes.

Maybe you'll find you can fly.

Earth Day

Climate change and other threats to the environment have become part of the global conversation in the last few years, and this is reflected in the growing popularity of books about the natural world.

And it's not just non-fiction, travel writing and memoir – there is even a new genre of fiction, cli-fi, where environmental issues play an important part in the story.

To celebrate World Earth Day on April 22nd here are some free-range writing ideas inspired by nature.

Memoir

Many of the most popular recent memoirs have as their theme the healing power of nature, either as a daily tonic or as a road to recovery from a major trauma such as bereavement, bankruptcy or addiction.

Think about times in your own life when you have felt inspired or consoled by nature, perhaps during a personal crisis but also in those small simple encounters with animals, birds, trees, flowers, stars, rainbows – any natural thing – that can happen any time and give your spirits a lift.

Jot down some ideas. Write about one or more of these occasions. Take fifteen minutes.

> TIP: Use all your senses to fully recall the scene. Senses are the key that unlocks memory and imagination, and describing how things feel, look, smell, taste and sound in your writing, can help readers to conjure them in imagination too.

Fiction

We are already feeling the catastrophic effects of climate change all over the world, including wildfires, floods, tsunamis, ice melts and rising sea levels. Threatened habitats are being placed under further pressure by pollution. This month, your free-range writing story will be a little piece of cli-fi, an intimate scene in an unfolding bigger story.

You can set it in the present or the imagined future. Two

people are trapped or imperilled by some kind of environmental disaster. What is the big picture – the unfolding situation in their neighbourhood, their country, their region of the world?

Make some notes about these two characters and the relationship between them. What's the history between them? What are their hopes for the future?

Pan in for a close-up. Where are they? How are they in danger? This is the moment when they will either survive or perish. Write the scene.

This is high drama, so don't be afraid of exaggerating. Write large. Take twenty minutes.

Non-Fiction

Greta Thunberg became a figurehead for climate action with her school strikes at the tender age of fifteen and she has become a powerful spokesperson on the world stage. I came across many other inspirational children and young people who are leading the way in their own communities when I was researching my book, 'How Can I Help the World?'

For this month's non-fiction foray, start with a bit of research yourself. Find five young people who are helping the planet in different ways, young inventors, conservationists, producers working with recycled materials... I can start you off with Elizabeth Gadson, 'the Little Collector', who began clearing litter in her neighbourhood on the Wirral when she was seven and has gone on to win many awards. You can read her story and see her in action on her facebook page TLC – Elizabeth: Caring for Wirral and the World

Choose one and write their story. Take ten minutes. If you're on social media, or they have a website with contact details, finish off by sending them a message of encouragement. Why not?

Poetry

What should we be doing to protect and save the world from climate catastrophe? Why should we care? Your poem this month is a call to action, written for performance, with the goal of inspiring an audience. To get in the zone with this, watch Amanda Gorman delivering her poem, 'The Hill We Climb', at President Biden's inauguration. Read the text too – it's freely available online. Notice the patterns of sound she uses – the internal rhyming, half rhymes, rhythms and alliterations.

When you draft your own poem, pay particular attention to what it sounds like, not just how it looks on the page – read it aloud at every stage. The ending is particularly important – that is your rallying call. A satisfying ending will often refer back to the beginning, so the poem makes a circle, and we can see the journey it has travelled. Gorman's starts with shade and closes with coming to light. Draft, redraft, play around with your ideas. Take about twenty minutes.

Unicorns

When it feels as if the walls are closing in on us in real life, we can always escape in imagination, and we do it naturally, without even noticing, daydreaming possible futures for ourselves, playing with different versions of the past.

So, fire up your imagination and go full fantasy with this month's free-range writing, because April 9th is National

Unicorn Day. Be playful, and enjoy your playfulness, because that is the essence of the first draft, whatever you are writing. As Brenda Ueland says in her book on becoming a writer, you shouldn't come to it feeling like a famous poet pontificating on a mountain top, but 'like a child in kindergarten, happily stringing beads.'

I think free-range writing is like that, playing with a theme, seeing what it does in different genres, and as you know there is only one rule – stick to the timings.

Memoir

In childhood, we encounter magical fantasy figures such as Father Christmas and the tooth fairy, and many children believe in dragons and unicorns and have imaginary friends. I was a more literal child, preferring adventure stories to elves and fairies, and staying awake to test my belief that Father Christmas was, in fact, my dad.

I've grown more open to fantasy fiction as I've got older; in fact, the first adult novel I sent to my agent was about aliens visiting the earth for their holidays.

How did you engage with magical figures in your childhood? Have you held the magic into adult life? How do you feel about fantasy books and films? Which ones have you enjoyed over the years? Write whatever comes, for twenty minutes.

Fiction

Some fantasy fiction is set in completely imagined worlds, but some simply introduces a fantasy element into a real world story, such as the alien in the family film, 'E.T,' or the humanoid amphibian in the romantic fantasy, 'The Shape of Water.'

Creating a whole new world is outside the scope of a twenty-minute free-range writing task, so your story here will be about a unicorn in a real life situation. Who sees or finds it? If you are writing for children, your protagonist will be the same age or slightly older than your reader. Make some character notes – their name, age, something about their circumstances.

A unicorn is a magical creature so, even if it needs rescuing, like the alien and the humanoid amphibian, it also has the power to bring positive change for the protagonist. What is wrong or missing in your protagonist's life? How can meeting the unicorn make their life better?

Jot down some notes about how the situation might develop. Perhaps this could be the beginning of many adventures, or a single longer story. Then write the scene of this magical first encounter, taking about fifteen minutes.

Non-Fiction

With sparkly unicorns featuring so strongly in books and clothes for small girls, you could be forgiven for thinking unicorns are just a commercial opportunity dreamed up by manufacturers and marketeers, but the unicorn has been around for centuries, across the globe.

It appeared in early Mesopotamian artworks, and in the ancient myths of India and China, where it was believed to have healing powers. In Christian mythology, it is a symbol for Christ and Mary. It was adopted as Scotland's national animal in the fifteenth century. In modern dating, it denotes... well if you don't know, you can find out!

Do some research. Write a list article of unicorn facts. Take twenty minutes.

> TIP: When you are writing an article, imagine it being published. What kind of magazine or website does it appear on? Picture it on the page. This will help you to visualise your reader and get the voice right.

Poetry

There's a poem that I like by David Hernandez called 'Sincerely, the Sky', in which the sky speaks to a person who often comes out onto their veranda at night and stares up at it. It starts, 'I see you there…'.and ends with the sky's advice to the stargazer. You can find the poem online.

The voice of your poem is a unicorn, speaking to a person who is looking at it in wonder, or maybe confusion, or happiness or shock. Start by imagining yourself as the unicorn, using all your senses. Fully inhabit that body; feel the air on your skin and in your nostrils, your four legs, your hooves, your strong back, your head, ears, mane. Your magical horn.

Imagine the scene where this encounter takes place. Picture the person, their body language, their face. Where are they? How old? Have they seen you before? Did they seek you out? What do you feel they need? What advice can you give them?

Write your poem, taking about twenty minutes.

Pets

National Pet Day is coming up in April. If you are a pet owner, it's a reminder to check your pet's health care is up to date, with vaccinations and so on, to clear out any toys that are no longer safe, update collar tags if you have changed your address and make sure your home is pet friendly.

For anyone who doesn't have a pet, it's a good time to think about other people – family, friends or neighbours – who may need help looking after their pets due to travel plans, old age or illness.

For writers, National Pet Day provides a great theme for a bit of free-range writing.

Memoir

Start with a list of pets, your own or other people's, from any period in your life. For me, that would include my grandmother's elderly Scottish Terrier, Scottie, then Patch, the puppy my father brought home in his coat pocket, my best friend's dog, my children's house rabbits and Sabre, the unfriendly Rottweiler that once lived next door.

Choose one. What did it look like? What noises did it make? What did it smell like? What did it feel like to touch or hold? Use all your senses and make some notes. Add some thoughts about its personality, and how you related to it emotionally.

Next, jot down some anecdotes from this animal's life – any funny, touching, exciting or worrying moments that come to mind. Choose one and tell the story. Take fifteen minutes.

Fiction

Pets can feel like family members, or important friends. This story will be about someone who either gains a pet or loses one, which can both be life-changing events. In my book, *Finding Fizz*, a little girl who is being bullied at school finds an orphaned puppy, and having someone even smaller and more vulnerable than she is helps her feel stronger and the teasing less important. In my Young Adult novel, *Drift,* the death of the dog is the first crack in the protagonist's sense of family as a safe and loving place.

In your story, who gains or loses a pet? Write a character sketch – name and age, physical description, likes and dislikes, situation. Make some notes about the pet as well – what kind of animal it is, its name, age and temperament.

What is your main character's life like before they gain or lose their pet? That's the beginning. How do they find or lose it? That's the action. In what way is their life different afterwards? That's the ending.

Write the story. Take twenty minutes.

Non-Fiction

Write a picture book text for young children about how to look after a pet. Most picture books are about 30 pages long, with a sentence or two of writing on each page, and part of the task is to make an artwork note where information can be conveyed in the illustration rather than spelt out in the text.

The easiest subject to choose is a pet you have looked after yourself – for me, that might be rabbits, fancy rats or hens. Then you won't need to do any research. What sort of housing does this animal need? What food? And health care? How can you look after its emotional needs?

Take ten minutes for a quick first draft, to get the content. Then take another ten to check the language, making sure it's pitched at a level that young children can understand, with no long sentences. You can include some words that might be unfamiliar, such as 'hutch' or 'dog basket' if the picture shows the reader what they mean.

> TIP: Writing for different readerships such as very young children is good practice for making you really think about your reader, what they will understand and be interested to know.

Poetry

In this poem, the narrator is either a pet owner talking about their pet or a pet talking about its owner.

Get some background first by imagining both the person and the pet, their names, ages and personalities; their physical attributes and how they feel about living with each other. Write some notes.

Which one feels more interesting to you, the owner or the animal? That will be your narrator. Especially if you are choosing the animal, you might consider making your poem rhyme for comic effect but keep it free verse if that feels more natural. Take fifteen minutes. Remember to give your poem a title.

> TIP: Because poems feel personal, we often assume they represent the poet's own experiences, thoughts and feelings. Writing poems from a fictional point of view like this can also help us to let go of such assumptions when we come to other people's poetry as readers.

MAY

Walking

May is National Walking Month – and walking is one of the best ways to get your creative ideas flowing.

Walking gets you out of the house and away from the desk. It makes you shift your attention, look up, look around. Like meditation, a good walk steadies your breathing and heart rate and clears your mind so that new insights can come in.

Too boring? Boring is good! Nature abhors a vacuum, and when you make empty time away from all your screens, books and to-do lists, fresh ideas come rushing in.

So why not try pondering these free-range writing forays on a ten-minute stroll before you sit down to write? Remember the rule when it comes to the actual writing though – stick to the timings!

Fiction

Two people are having a walk together. Who? What is the relationship between them? Where are they walking? Have they done this walk before? Make some notes.

The relationship is under some kind of strain. What's the problem? Is it a recent thing, or deeply embedded? More notes!

One of them says something that upsets the other.

Write the conversation between them, embedding the dialogue in the action. 'She said, opening the gate…',' A pigeon flapped up from the bushes…', 'He looked away.'

Take about twenty minutes.

> TIP: When you're writing dialogue, don't only think about what the people are saying. Picture the whole scene. Focus on the action and let the dialogue unfold within it.

Memoir

Have you ever really needed to get out and go for a walk, to calm down after an argument, for example, or think about a problem, or have a break from the kids or work off a hangover? Jot down a few examples from different stages in your life.

Choose one to write about. What was your emotional and physical state when you set out? Where did you experience your emotions in your body? How did you feel different by the time you got back?

Write the story. Take twenty minutes. If you finish early, write about another example from your list.

Non-Fiction

Write an article giving instructions about a walk around your local area. 'Start at the car park in Frederick Street...' and so on.

This could be a famous, scenic walk taking in some interesting sights, but it doesn't have to be. It could be a little-known short cut or suggested exercise circuit. You could make it humorous or ironic – one memorable walk I once did, following a leaflet from the tourist office, included 'the beautiful sewage treatment works' where, on a still day, one might enjoy the rich natural aromas rising from it.

When you have finished, read back over your article and give it a title. Under the title, indicate the main points of interest, estimated walking time and level of difficulty.

You can add a fact box if you like, such as possible places to park the car, or get refreshments along the way.

Twenty minutes.

> TIP: If you decide to send it off to a walking magazine/website, do the walk to check what you've written first. I once wrote a children's book about a walk in Fair Isle, working from maps – but when I tried to do the walk on a visit to the island, I got completely lost!

Poetry

Re-read your memoir piece.

Write the story of that walk as a poem. Don't use a set rhythm or pattern of rhyme unless the poem seems to demand it – if you were marching, or plodding, for example.

Start by simply describing the walk – remembering the details, what you saw and heard; the weather and time of day; the smell of the air and the feel of the ground beneath your feet.

Stick to the physical experience of the walk and the environment; only move on into thoughts and feelings about the walk if they begin to arise naturally out of that. Take about twenty minutes.

> TIP: Julia Cameron, author of one of the most popular books for writers ever written, *The Artist's Way*, offers walking as her third major recommendation, along with morning pages and the artist's date. You can read all about it in her book, *Walking in This World: Spiritual Strategies for Forging Your Creative Trail*.

Mental Health

Mental Health Awareness week falls in May. From children in school to princes of the realm, people are far more willing to talk about their own struggles nowadays, so we are more aware than we used to be of the huge problem we have across society with mental health issues such as stress, loneliness and depression.

At the same time, we're beginning to see robust research findings that confirm the incredible benefits of any kind of creative practice. As little as twenty minutes of writing a couple of times a week, on any subject, has been shown not just to improve people's mental wellbeing but even their physical health as well.

Writing is a 'flow' activity – it absorbs all your attention and makes you lose track of time. So this month, as you free-range across the different genres, notice how writing lifts you away from the cares of the day.

And remember, stick to the timings!

Memoir

A diary can feel like a dear and trusted friend, and many people turn to diary-writing at times of particular stress and difficulty. Anne Frank gave her diary a name and started each day, 'Dear Kitty...'

Write a diary entry beginning 'Dear Diary.' Tell your diary – real or imagined – about your day today or yesterday, or any recent experiences you have had, or anything that is currently making you feel happy or unhappy.

Take twenty minutes. Finish by signing off and saying thank you to your diary for being there.

> TIP: Writing helps relieve loneliness, because it provides a sense of connection, even when the person you are connecting with is yourself.

Fiction

Stories always start with a problem and arrive at a solution. If your protagonist is perfectly happy and nothing bad happens, there is no challenge and no story.

So, in this story, someone has a problem. Who? What is their problem? For example, he or she might be worried about their health; they might have fallen out with a family member; they might be feeling lonely…

How might they try to solve the problem? Jot down some ideas. She plucks up the courage to go to the doctor; he picks up the phone; she offers to walk her sick neighbour's dog… Choose one of the things they might try, and take twenty minutes to write the scene.

Whether they succeed or fail, either way, they will have moved things on. In a story, as in life, effort and action always brings, at the very least, the benefit of experience.

> TIP: If you give one of your own problems to your protagonist, writing their story can be a great way of exploring your options.

Non-Fiction

Why might creative writing bring relief from social, psychological and emotional problems? Jot down some ideas. For example, it means taking time out for yourself, it's a chance to explore your thoughts and emotions, it's a skill you can enjoy developing...

In what ways do you feel writing boosts your own mental health and wellbeing? Can you think of specific examples? Have you ever found writing in a group situation to have similar positive effects? More notes.

How might you develop your writing practice to maximise the wellbeing benefits? Be specific; where? When? If with other people, who? Make more notes!

Then write a personal piece – 'My writing and me' – about your relationship with writing both in the past and present day and also for your imagined future. Take fifteen minutes.

> **TIP**: If you are interested in writing for therapy or self-development, check out the international organisation, Lapidus: The Writing for Wellbeing Community.

Poetry

Write a list of emotions – joy, enthusiasm, jealousy, anger... When you've got ten, choose one, and underline it.

With this emotion in mind, think of an animal. Go with the first idea that pops into your head.

Now, forget about the emotion – put it completely out of your mind – and write some notes about the animal, how it looks, sounds, smells and moves. If it isn't an animal that you know a lot about, get in the zone with a spot of research. Find some images – notice the body language, imagine how it would feel to be inside that body.

Write a poem about the animal. Start by focusing on

simply describing it and then, if you want to, round it off with some kind of personal response at the end. What do you think or feel about the animal?

You can choose to keep it free or choose a regular pattern of rhythm and rhyme, depending upon which way feels right for your subject. Take twenty minutes.

> TIP: Try this when you feel sad, bored or anxious. Finding an image for how you feel is a way of creating distance and looking at it from outside.

Dying Matters

For decades, death has felt like a taboo subject, but that is changing. Psychological studies suggest that thinking about death ('mortality salience') can lift your happiness and self-esteem, help you be less money-orientated and even make you funnier. It's also good from a pragmatic point of view, to plan for your own death, for the sake of those you will leave behind.

Dying Matters Awareness Week falls in May, so this is a good time to get to grips with the theme of death in some free-range writing forays. Don't be afraid to cry, and don't be afraid to laugh either. Just go where the writing takes you and let yourself be surprised.

Memoir

The English language has 200 euphemisms for death – that's how reluctant we have been to talk about it, but you can find lots of chat about it in social media especially around Dying Matters Awareness Week, when people share information and personal stories involving death, dying and grief.

What personal stories could you share? Have you lost somebody you loved? Have you had a brush with death yourself? Do you remember where you were when Princess Diana died, or Elvis, or JFK? Did you see footage of the Queen, sitting alone at her husband's funeral during the Covid lockdowns? Did you hear the tribute to Meat Loaf played at the changing of the guards?

What are your views about public mourning? What private fears might you like to talk about? How could your experiences help someone else?

Write whatever comes for twenty minutes. If one thought stream peters out, simply take a new direction. You're not trying to write elegant prose but simply to explore the theme through writing.

Fiction

The scene is a death café, where strangers meet to enjoy tea and cakes, and chat about death (Death Café is an international movement based on the idea that talking about death helps people make the most of their lives.)

Your protagonist has come because he or she wants to talk about death. Why? Why Now? Why here, among strangers? Why can't they talk to a family member or friend? Make some character notes including their name, age, something about their appearance and their circumstances.

The event opens with everyone introducing themselves and, if they wish, sharing the reasons why they have come. The protagonist doesn't open up to the whole group but engages in conversation later with one other person.

Who? How does the conversation go? How does it help?
Write the scene. Take twenty minutes.

Non-Fiction

One of the benefits of thinking about your own death is that it helps you appreciate the small things in life right now and stop putting off the bigger ones you want to do in the future. As nobody has forever, it pays to have a plan.

Write a list of all the things you would like to do, from big ones such as going on safari or publishing a novel to smaller ones such as trying the new tea shop on the high street. Jot your ideas down, just as they come.

Choose one of your big ideas and break it down into steps. What needs to be done, in order for it to happen? What could you do right now, to set the wheels in motion?

Choose one of your smaller ideas and schedule a time to do it in the next few weeks.

How does this way of thinking make you feel? In theory, it should make you feel more energised and focused, but perhaps, for you, it brings unhappiness and panic instead. Or it could be a bit of both. Write your personal response for five minutes, reflecting what effect greater 'mortality salience' might have on the way you live your life.

Poetry

One of the readings at Princess Diana's funeral was a very moving poem by Mary Lee Hall, called 'Turn again to life.' It begins, 'If I should die…' You can find it online.

What would you like to say to the people you leave behind, in the event of your death? What message would you have for your loved ones, or for the world? You can make it serious and heartfelt, like 'Turn again to life', but there is also an opportunity here for humour, like Spike Milligan's epitaph, 'I told you I was ill.'

Write a poem beginning, 'If I should die...' Mary Lee Hall's poem is just eight lines, with a regular pattern of rhythm and rhyme – ABBACDDC – and that is an option you might consider for your poem. Rhyming may be a good choice, especially if you are going for humour.

Take about twenty minutes.

Biscuits

National Biscuit Day comes up in May and we have a wonderful variety of biscuits to celebrate, from workaday plain digestives to classy chocolate shortcakes and the classic, custard creams.

Writing is a way of paying attention to life in all its details and using your senses to recreate experiences in imagination or create new ones. It's all about pleasure and discovery.

Increase your writing pleasure, if you'd like to, with a cup of tea and a favourite biscuit as you tuck into this month's free-range writing – or why not take a walk on the wild side and try a kind you've never tasted before? That's living creatively!

Memoir

Jot down the names of some of the biscuits you associate with different periods in your life, or with specific occasions. In my early childhood, that would be garibaldis, otherwise known as 'dead fly biscuits', and those plain round ones with bumpy tops that I only discovered recently are called Lincoln biscuits.

On Scottish holidays when my children were young, it was Tunnocks teacakes. These days, I give my writing groups a selection of fancy Foxes.

Choose a kind of biscuit from your list to write about. If possible, eat one; if not, imagine eating it. Take your time. Start your writing by describing the taste, smell, appearance and texture of the biscuit and recalling the period in your life you associate it with.

Then tell the story of a particular occasion when you ate one of those biscuits, starting this section, 'Once...'. If you can't remember the precise details, such as time and place, feel free to go with your best guess. Take twenty minutes.

Fiction

Somebody gives someone a biscuit. Maybe they are buying one for a grandchild, a friend, a homeless stranger, or offering one as comfort for an anxious patient, or handing round refreshments at a funeral, village concert, evening class...

Who is giving? Who is receiving? What is the relationship between them? Where is this happening? What is the occasion? Make some notes on the characters and setting.

Food is nourishment, and the giving of food can be an expression of friendship or love, but it may not always be well received. How confident is the giver of the reaction they will get? What is the receiver's first response? How could you use this little interaction to show us something about the characters and their relationship, without spelling it out? Tell the story. Take about fifteen minutes.

> TIP: 'Show don't tell' means instead of saying how people are feeling – 'He was fed up with his mother. She was doing his head in' – you let their actions show it. 'He shoved the packet back at her. "I've told you a hundred times, I hate that kind of biscuit!"'

Non-Fiction

In your opinion, what are the five best kinds of biscuits? What are the five worst? Top of my best list would be Foxes triple choc chunky; top of my worst, Jaffa cakes (I know – controversial!')

Write a list piece, justifying your choices with a sentence or two about each one. 'Foxes triple choc chunkie. Great crumbly texture chocolatey base with big chunks of dark and white chocolate, so you don't have to choose between them – you get both.'

Jaffa cakes. Unpleasant texture. Also, marmalade has no place in a biscuit.

Gingernuts. Amazing dunkers but should carry a health warning for those of mature years with bridges and fillings.

Take twenty minutes.

Poetry

There's a lovely little poem by William Carlos Williams called 'This is Just to Say' – it reads like a note from the poet apologising for eating all the plums in the fridge. You can find it online if you are not familiar with it.

Call your poem, 'The Last Biscuit', and imagine it scrawled on a piece of paper, lying among the last crumbs on an empty plate or in an empty tin. Address it to someone you live with or have lived with at some stage in the past.

Can you use the tone and content of the poem to suggest what kind of relationship you have or used to have with each other – warm, funny, sexy, frosty, resentful…

If you prefer, make the person who leaves the note and the person they are leaving it for fictional characters. What is the relationship between them? Write your poem in the first person, 'I', as the biscuit eater.

Or you could play with the idea a little bit more and write a poem about what happened from the point of view of the plate or tin. Try to give the plate or tin some personality and a point of view about the eating of the last biscuit.

As these will all be very short, try lots of versions. Take ten or fifteen minutes.

JUNE

Reading Groups

Free-range writing across different genres helps you go off your normal writing tracks and become a more adventurous writer. If you want to become a more adventurous reader too, why not join a reading group? National Reading Group Day in June could be the perfect time to do it.

Ask in your local library or bookshop; check out the reading groups website or simply get together with a few friends and start one up yourself.

Reading other people's book choices is a great way of discovering new writers, genres or subjects you might never have thought of trying on your own. Also, chatting about books is an opportunity to share much more of your thoughts, ideas and feelings than you might in other social situations.

But before you go rushing out to find a reading group, get in the zone with these free-range writing forays.

Memoir

Write a list of books you have loved at different times in your life.

Choose three and write a few sentences about why you loved each one and how you might feel if you read it again now.

Choose one of those three. Close your eyes and imagine yourself back in the time and place where you first read it. For example, a book I loved was *The Writer's Journey*, by Christopher Vogler, and I read it on a series of beaches in the Scillies twenty years ago.

Feel the weight of the book in your hands. Use your

senses to immerse yourself in your surroundings. How did reading this book make you feel? What did you learn? Who did you talk to about it? Write about the book, the place and time in your life when you read it, and what it meant to you. Take ten minutes.

Fiction

Imagine a reading group of four individuals. Are they male or female? Are they different ages? Where do they meet? How long have they been meeting for? Do they know each other outside the group? Jot down some general notes.

Now make some character sketches of each one, including their name, age and something about their physical appearance. Do they have any health issues? What are their social situations, and how do they feel about their lives right now?

What kind of book would each of these characters choose for the reading group? Choose a specific title – if you can't name a particular cycling guide or medical romance or whatever other kind of book your characters are choosing, have a look in your local library, bookshop or online retailer. Your characters' choices of book will say a lot about them.

Take about 5 minutes for each of these character sketches. That's the task, but if you feel a story coming on, I wouldn't want to stop you! Take as long as you like.

> TIP: Asking your characters about their favourite books/ TV shows/foods/shops and so on is a great way to develop your sense of who they are.

Non-Fiction

Make a list of five books you think would work well for a reading group. Write a few sentences about each one, first describing it and then explaining why you think it would be a good choice for a reading group – for example, the controversial theme would spark discussion, or it's a short easy read.

Don't just think in terms of current bestsellers that everyone will have heard of. A reading group is an opportunity to discover lesser-known books, and genres such as non-fiction, poetry, Young Adult and even children's books that many readers wouldn't normally think of choosing. Take about twenty minutes.

Poetry

Choose a book from your bookshelves at home to write about. If haven't got any books around the house, pop down to your local library and choose one. If you're already in a reading group, go with the book you are all reading at the moment.

Hold the book in your hands. Notice its physical properties – its weight and thickness, age and cover style. Does it have a smell? Flick through the pages, thinking about what it contains. What will readers find in these pages? What won't they find?

Notice how this book makes you feel emotionally. What does it mean to you? Why have you chosen it?

Write a poem describing the book, its physical properties and content. Finish with a personal observation or response to it. Take twenty minutes.

> TIP: You don't have to know what the ending or point of a poem will be before you start. Focus on simply describing an object, and you will find that thoughts and ideas gradually firm up around it.

Father's Day

Free-range writing is personal writing – no one else will ever read it, and that makes it a safe space for exploring topics that could spark strong emotions. Father's Day falls in June and whatever your relationship with your own father or the men who have been father figures in your life, writing about fathers could get emotional.

Don't be afraid to feel the feelings. As the American poet Robert Frost said, 'No tears in the writer, no tears in the reader.' If what you feel is mostly love and gratitude, enjoy it. If it's more complicated or negative, take a step back after you have written and reflect that you are more than your relationship with your father – it is only one aspect in the kaleidoscope of experiences that make up your life.

Memoir
Write a list of men who have been father figures to you, perhaps briefly or perhaps over many years. This could include your father, stepfather, godfather, father-in-law, other family member, teacher, mentor, male friend…

For example, when I was in my teens, a family friend, Uncle Don, took me to art exhibitions and nurtured creative ambitions in me that my own parents could not understand. When my relationship with my own father broke down, my psychiatrist was like a kindly father. Others in my life include my junior school headteacher and the choirmaster who, although a little younger than me, brought stability and wisdom into my life when I needed it in my early fifties.

Choose one. Think about when and why he was important to you, and the difference he has made in your life, which might be positive or negative.

Write a letter to him, reflecting on your relationship, including specific memories. Tell him what you really feel. This is personal writing in an epistolary form – you aren't going to send it!

Take twenty minutes. If you need less than that for the first one, move on and do a second one.

> TIP: As with all personal writing, you might discover ideas you would like to work up into a finished piece that would be sharable – in this case, a letter you could send.

Fiction

In George Eliot's novel, *Silas Marner*, a small child arrives at the door of an isolated old man on a snowy night. Retracing her footsteps in the snow, he discovers the body of her mother, so he has no choice but to take the child in. It's an uplifting story about the transformational power of fatherly love, for both the father figure and the child. The blockbuster film 'About a Boy' explores the same idea.

In your story, a childless man finds himself in a situation where somebody, either a child or an adult, needs a father figure. At first, make your protagonist reluctant to step up. Why does he hold back, and what makes him decide to engage? How does this relationship change both the father figure and the other character?

Take twenty minutes.

Non-Fiction

Father's Day and Mother's Day began as religious festivals celebrating the Christian forefathers, the mother church, the virgin mother, but evolved into more secular celebrations of personal mothers and fathers to reflect changes in society.

When I was growing up, virtually every child in my school had a mother and a father, but these days many children live in blended families, or single parent families or have same-sex parents, so is the way we celebrate Mother's Day and Father's Day still relevant?

Write an opinion piece on how you think we could celebrate Mother's Day and Father's Day in a way that feels more inclusive for every child in the modern world. Take twenty minutes.

Poetry

Find an old photo that includes your father or another father figure in your life. Write in prose for three minutes, describing everything you see in the photo. 'A young man is sitting on a garden wall. He is wearing... he looks... Behind him, the cottage is...'

Focus in on your father/father figure – what is he feeling? Is there information in his body language? Copy his pose with your own body. How does it feel?

Google these two poems for inspiration: 'On Finding an Old Photograph' by Wendy Cope, and 'Photograph of My Father in His Twenty-Third Year' by Raymond Carver. They both begin with descriptions of a photo of their father and end with a closing reflection.

Write a poem about your photo following the same pattern. Take twenty minutes.

Knitting

Worldwide Knit in Public Day falls on the second Saturday in June, when knitting enthusiasts gather in parks and gardens, libraries and cafes to celebrate their craft.

There are nearly seven and a half million knitters in the UK, including national figures such as Kate Middleton and Olympic champion Tom Daley, and lots of people learnt to knit during the coronavirus lockdowns, including me.

As National Writing Day also falls in June, this month's knitting-themed free-range writing ticks all the boxes.

Memoir

I was a child in the 1950's, when girls learnt to knit at school, and most of our clothes were home-made. Even our swimming costumes were knitted, which is not something I can recommend!

What hand knitted garments do you recall from different periods in your life, perhaps knitted by you or a family member or friend? Include any hand-knitted garments you have bought – for me that might include the Fair Isle hat I bought when I was camping in Shetland a few years ago. If you haven't owned any hand-knitted garments, think of favourite sweaters and cardigans you have worn over the years. Make some notes.

Choose one, and write a description of it, using all your

senses to describe it. Remember what it felt like on your body. Take three minutes. Then think of specific occasions when you wore it and jot them down. What happened to it, where is it now? What does your fondness for this garment say about you, and that period in your life? Another three minutes.

Write for about ten minutes, on the history of that garment in your life. Notice how using all the senses to recall an object from your past – something you wore, something you ate, something you listened to – can bring the past vividly back to you.

Fiction

Someone has died and a friend or family member is clearing out their house. They find a half-finished piece of knitting. What is it? Are they surprised to find it?

They decide to finish it. Think about the time scale – will it be a single knitting session, or something they will stop and start many times over an extended period? Write the story of them finishing the knitting and include a story-within-a-story, of a memory about the deceased person that comes back to them as they work. Try to give both a sense of the protagonist's current circumstances and the history of the relationship between them and the deceased.

End with them finishing the garment. How have their feelings changed, between finding the half-finished knitting and holding the completed article? Is there a healing power in knitting? Take twenty minutes.

Non-Fiction

As there so many knitters in the UK, the chances are you know some, either in the real world or in your social networks, and this week's non-fiction task is an interview with a knitter. Plan the questions you want to ask but remember to make space for them to add anything they want to say outside your questions. Take as long as you like for the interview, but no more than twenty minutes for the actual writing. Start with a sentence or two of introduction about the knitter and round it off with a sentence or two in conclusion.

If you are a knitter, you could interview yourself, introducing yourself in the third person and then writing the interview as a simple Q and A. If you aren't a knitter and don't know anyone who is, write an interview with yourself on that. There might be an opportunity for humour!

Poetry

Imagine you are reading an article in a glossy magazine about Worldwide Knit in Public Day. It includes a full-page photo of a group of people knitting together in a public space. Whereabouts in the world are they? What kind of space – indoors or outdoors? What season and time of day or night? Are there people in the background who are not part of the knitting group?

Notice the colours and the way the photo is composed. What is the general feeling of the image? Do any of the individual knitters draw your particular interest? Close or lower your eyes and fully imagine it.

Write a poem describing what you see in the picture – the setting and the group and then, if you like, focus in one individual within it. Finish with a reflection – what thoughts or feelings does the image inspire in you? Take twenty minutes.

> TIP: You could share fragments of this writing on social media on World Knit in Public Day, using the hashtag #KnitInPublicDay or #WWKIPDAY.

Writing Day

National Writing Day falls in June, and what better way to celebrate than with a burst of free-range writing? The fact that no-one else is going to read it releases you from any pressure to write well, so it's a great opportunity to try new things and go outside your comfort zone.

Of course, as a bonus, there's always a chance your personal writing might turn up something you'd like to develop further, so it can become a seedbed for projects you will go on to publish or share in the future.

Short, timed pieces mean you don't have a chance to overthink – you're writing on instinct, and that takes you straight to the heart of what matters to you right now, which is where the creative energy is. Check it out with these free-range ideas, on the theme of writing itself.

Memoir

Start with the prompt, 'I remember...' and write for fifteen minutes. Let your mind go where it wants to, not trying to stick to any kind of chronological order. Repeat the prompt as often as you like, whenever you find yourself going off in a new direction.

Read back over what you have written. Is there a dominant emotional tone or theme? Have you drawn on memories from a particular stage in your life, or about particular people or places? Does anything in your choice of material surprise you?

If this glimpse into your past was a colour, what colour would it be? How would you describe that colour? For example, your particular green could be vibrant or muddy, your pink could be warm or artificial.

Change the colour and write memories with a different emotional tone for another five minutes, beginning 'I remember'.

> TIP: Writing memoir is an opportunity to recover parts of your past that memory has filtered out. If you think of yourself as having had a generally sunny childhood, you may rediscover the darker moments; if you feel your past was unremittingly dark, you will find the sunnier ones.

Fiction

Books, articles, letters – they can all be a source of great comfort or insight at difficult times in our lives. For example, a murder mystery series could give you something else to think about during a spell in hospital, or a memoir of loss feel like an understanding friend when you're going through a bereavement.

I once had an email from a reader who told me that my children's book, *Bullies, Bigmouths and So-called Friends* had helped her realise she could walk away from her 'so-called boyfriend'. 'I'm actually 27 years old,' her message began, and then she told me the whole story.

Your story will take the form of a letter or email from a reader to the author of something they have read that helped them solve a problem or get through a difficult time. Write a few notes about this character and their situation. The author they are writing to could be a real author and a real book, or a made-up character like your protagonist.

Imagine you are your protagonist and write the letter or email. Tell the author what was going on for you and how their work helped or inspired you. Take twenty minutes.

Non-Fiction

When has a book, article or blog post helped or inspired you? Jot down a few ideas. James Morton's bread book has inspired my whole family to start baking this year and I'm loving the way that punctuating my writing morning with working on the dough creates little pockets of mental space for new ideas to come in.

You know what's coming! Check out your author's website or social media and send them a message, thanking them for their work and saying what it has meant for you. Alternatively, write a review and post it on an online retailer's website, or on your own social media. This may take five minutes of your time and make their day.

Celebrating each other's writing is just as important as enjoying and valuing our own. Be generous. What goes around comes around.

Poetry

Ted Hughes describes the process of writing poetry as being like hunting or fishing, patiently waiting with all his senses on high alert. An idea is like a fox; a mind is like a pond full of fish that we need to find own way of catching.

I'm a dreamer, not a hunter, and I think of the process of writing as being like creative dreaming, where you set an intention before you go to sleep and receive the insight you were looking for in your dreams. First the focus, then the wait, then the capture.

For your poem, use one of your own hobbies or interests as an image for your writing process. Maybe you enjoy baking, or gardening, or singing in a choir – you could choose anything but be specific.

Not just baking generally, but baking what? Growing which plant? Singing which song? This will help you to use all your senses and anchor your poem. Read 'The Thought Fox' by Ted Hughes to see how effective this can be. Take twenty minutes.

JULY

Friendship

There's a lovely celebration day in July every year – the International Day of Friendship. It was officially recognised by the UN in 2011 to highlight the importance of strong ties and trust in a world so often torn apart by conflict.

People need to feel connected, and writing creates feelings of connection even when we're doing it just for ourselves. In fiction, we connect with the characters we create; they come alive for us because of the way they make us feel.

In non-fiction, we connect with the ideas and experiences that spark our interest and passion; in poetry, we connect with the symbolic layer of the psyche, where meaning is not objective and exact, but something the heart understands.

Every kind of writing connects us with our shared humanity and helps us feel and appreciate the rich complicatedness of our shared human condition.

So connect up this month with these free-range writing ideas and, if you like, share one with a writing friend on International Friendship Day, July 30th

Memoir

A friend in need is a friend indeed...

When did you really need a friend? Jot down a few examples. Choose one.

Did you reach out for help? Who was there for you?

Write the story. Ten minutes.

When were you there for somebody else? You might find it harder to think of examples, because we tend to remember other people's kindness more readily than our own.

Choose one and write the story. Ten minutes.

> TIP: Memoir isn't just about childhood, and a memoir doesn't have to start in childhood and tell the writer's whole life story. You can find great stories to write about from every stage of your life, right up to the present moment.

Fiction

Someone is feeling left out.

- Who, where and why? For example, a scholarship boy in an expensive school because his family is poor, or a new employee in a coffee shop because she doesn't speak the language.
- Their way of coping with feeling left out is making matters worse. How? Write some notes about the character and their situation.
- Someone holds out the hand of friendship to them. Who? More notes.
- How do they respond?

Decide whose point of view feels more interesting to you, the one who feels left out, or the one who tries to help them. Write the scene, as that character, in the first person, 'I...'

Twenty minutes.

Non-Fiction

Imagine you have been commissioned to write a very short piece for a greetings card company's website using International Friendship Day to promote their selection of cards for friends.

Begin by doing a bit of research. Although it was officially recognised by the UN in 2011, International Friendship Day has its roots a long time before that, and it's celebrated in different ways and on different dates in different countries.

Learning new things is one of the great joys of writing non-fiction, especially now that it's so easy with online search engines. Take ten minutes, and jot down any facts you find interesting.

Once you've gathered some background information, decide what you want to include in your article. Remember who you're writing it for, and that it has to be very short, two or three paragraphs at most. The challenge with any piece of writing is deciding what to include and what to leave out especially with work that includes a lot of research, such as non-fiction and historical fiction.

Take about twenty minutes for the research and the writing.

> TIP: A quick online search is fine for personal non-fiction writing, but before you publish a piece of non-fiction you should always crosscheck several sources, as anyone can post anything online and, even in books, information can quickly go out of date.

Poetry

Write the names of five friends, from any stage of your life, just the first ones that come to you. These may include animals that have felt like friends to you.

Choose which one you'd like to write about.

Write a poem, describing the first time you ever laid eyes

on them. Where were you? Who else was there? What was your first impression? Keep it free, so you can really focus on your description, and not be distracted by having to make it fit into a fixed rhythm or rhyming pattern.

When you have finished describing the first time you met, make a transition beginning 'And now…' or 'But now…' and go on to describe how your friendship has developed since that first meeting.

Take twenty minutes. If you finish early, use the rest of the time to try different versions, or different ways of laying it out on the page.

> TIP: A poem is just a short piece of writing, set out on the page so that it looks like a poem. Its small scope means both poet and reader can give special attention to the richness and musicality of the language and the resonance of the ideas and images.

Seaside

We are an island nation and nowhere in the UK is more than seventy miles from coastal waters so, when the warm weather comes, our thoughts often turn to the sea.

If you can't get down to the coast and soak up the sound and smell of the sea, you can still enjoy some beach time in memory and imagination with this month's free-range writing.

So breathe in the salty air, listen to the waves, feel the warmth of the sun on your skin… and write! The only thing you have to remember is this: stick to the timings.

Memoir

The way to bring your memories to life is by focusing on the senses, and beach days are always a feast of sensations.

Make a list of beach days you remember from different periods of your life. Choose one to write about. Thinking about a specific occasion, what was the weather like? The time of day? Who else was there?

What could you see? Notice the colours and movement – both up close in detail and moving gradually out into the distance.

What could you hear? Again, think close by and far away.

What could you smell or taste – close by, perhaps the coconut sun cream on your arms or your rum and raisin ice cream; in the wider environment, perhaps the waft of chips from the beach café or the salty sea air.

What could you feel? The sun on your skin or the chilly breeze... the fine sand between your toes or the shifting pebbles...

Write a description using all your senses. Take as long as you like – some writers will find this much easier than others. Don't feel self-conscious about whether it's any good – you're simply using writing as a way of recovering a past experience.

Repeat with other beach days on your list, up to a total time of twenty minutes.

Fiction

Summer is the perfect time for a little light-hearted holiday romance. Picture, in your mind, the beach reads display in a bookshop window to get you in the mood.

Think about some beaches you have visited, either here or overseas. Choose one to use for your setting, and jot down a few notes, using all your senses.

What kind of person would come to this beach? Not everyone who loves the bustle of Brighton would enjoy the wild solitude of Sandwood Bay. Imagine someone standing or sitting there, all alone. Notice their clothes and body language. What are they thinking and feeling? More notes, including their name and age.

In fiction, the protagonist always wants something and, in romance, that something is love. What has happened in your character's life that has brought them to this moment of longing? More notes!

Bring a second character onto the beach who is also looking for love and then, play Cupid. Make something happen on the beach that causes these two people to strike up a conversation or take some kind of action together. A lost child is looking for their parents... A rescue helicopter is hovering over the sea... Someone is playing their music at top volume...

Write the scene. Take fifteen minutes.

Non-Fiction

One kind of non-fiction is the personal recount: telling the story of what happened to you as a way of conveying information. Write a personal recount of a trip you have made to a beach. Think in terms of your target reader – for example, families, retirees, keen walkers, post-exam teens. What aspects of your experience would they be particularly interested in?

Add an information box including things that aren't in your recount, such as how to get there, parking, top tips, safety warnings, facilities...

Take twenty minutes.

Poetry

I once read this report in my local paper: 'WI competition for the strangest object found on a beach: First prize, Mrs K Stanbury'!

What strange objects have you found on a beach? Near Wick, I found the bare branch of a tree that someone had stood up in the sand and festooned with washed up rubber gloves that, from a distance, looked like leaves. On Balnakiel beach, I found a person I thought was dead, but it turned out he was dead drunk.

Write a poem about a strange object you have found on a beach – if you can't think of one, use your imagination. Name and describe the beach and use all your senses to embed your object in the setting. Take twenty minutes.

Check out these two fine flotsam and jetsam poems if you need some inspiration – 'The Beach' by Kathleen Jamie and 'Beachcomber' by George Mackay Brown.

Plastic

Plastic's fantastic, it's cheap to manufacture, endlessly versatile and virtually indestructible, but all its advantages are precisely why it has become a global problem. Plastic Free July is dedicated to raising awareness and finding solutions.

Whatever your first reaction to the idea of Plastic Free July, see whether writing about it in different genres softens and develops your thinking. Free-range writing isn't just about making your writing more interesting; it makes life more interesting too.

Memoir

Because plastic is so cheap and easy to produce, we don't value it in the same way as things made of traditional materials and we treat every plastic thing as short-term and disposable. If we valued plastic items more, perhaps we would hold onto them, make less plastic and throw less away.

What plastic things have you used, re-used and valued in your life, even though you could easily and cheaply have replaced them? I've used the same travel soapbox for all my trips in recent years. It's a plain, unprepossessing thing, but functional, and it carries memories for me of campsites and hotels and holiday lets in wonderful places. I bought a Tupperware for sandwiches in Torshavn that I've used every picnic since, and it always reminds me of the Faroes. I have three big plastic patio tubs that I cherish because my son gave them to me and they're beautifully designed.

If you can't think of any, what plastic things that you use today could you start to feel differently about now? Write for twenty minutes, just whatever comes, in appreciation of the plastic things in your life.

Fiction

Your story this month is about someone who has an epiphany moment, a sudden realisation that there is a plastic problem, and that they can do something about it. The legal ban on free plastic carrier bags in shops began with a filmmaker called Rebecca Hosking, a keen diver who was swimming among plastic carrier bags that floated like jellyfish all around her, when she suddenly decided she had to do something about it. She asked all the shopkeepers in her local town of Modbury to replace plastic carrier bags with ones made from recycled paper.

In Looe, where crabbing is very popular with families, the local community provide recycling crab-line bins to protect seabirds and fishes from getting entangled, and in some seaside places, families are invited to leave their buckets and spades in beach boxes at the end of their stay for other families to enjoy.

Where does your protagonist live? What plastic pollution problem could they suddenly feel sufficiently concerned about to feel they must do something? In an urban setting, it could be an incident in a park where they see litter that might present a danger to young children, or a fast-food outlet, where they see a rat among the rubbish.

Your story begins with them going about their normal activities, and then their ah-ha moment, when they fully notice a litter situation they've been walking past every day and suddenly realise 'This is not OK!'

Where are they? Use all your senses to set the scene. Who are they with if anyone? How do they feel emotionally when they have their epiphany moment? How do they experience those emotions in their body? Close your eyes and imagine it. Your story ends with their decision about what they're going to do. Take twenty minutes.

Non-Fiction

Everyone is aware of plastic rubbish littering beaches even in the farthest corners of the world, but what do you know about trash islands? I had never heard of them until I researched *How Can I Help the World?*, my green book for older children a few years ago, and I was shocked.

Do some research online; research is one of the pleasures

of writing non-fiction. Many respondents in a survey about happiness I read when I was working on *How to be Happy* reported they found learning new things more pleasurable than sex!

Write a piece about trash islands. This can be a numbered list of facts – the what, why, when, where and how of trash islands – or an opinion piece, how you feel about them, broadening out to your feelings about plastic pollution more generally. Take twenty minutes.

Poetry

There's a poem by the Orkney poet, George Mackay Brown, called 'Beachcomber', where he itemises objects he's found on the beach, starting with an old boot on Monday, then a piece of timber on Tuesday, and so on through the week.

He was writing in the 1970s and all the objects he mentions are made from natural materials. Now, if you go beach combing, you're more likely to find every different kind of plastic trash, tangled up in the seaweed and strewn across the sand.

Write your own contemporary poem, called 'Beachcomber.' Check out George Mackay Brown's poem online if you'd like to first, for inspiration. End your poem, as he does, with a personal reflection. Take twenty minutes.

Staycations

Coronavirus lockdowns in recent years shut down global travel and forced everyone to think more locally when it came to planning holidays. How lucky for us that we live in a country with an amazing variety of landscapes, fascinating towns and beautiful villages to explore.

Celebrate the Great British staycation with July's free-range writing.

Memoir

Jog your memory about some of the summer trips and holidays you have taken in the UK by looking through old photographs. Choose one that draws you today.

What did it feel like in that moment when the photograph was taken? Use all your senses to fully recall the scene. Take your time.

What does it feel like now, looking at this photo? Notice how you are experiencing the emotions in your body.

Write about that holiday generally, then the moment of the photograph and finally how you feel about it now, looking back. Take about twenty minutes.

Fiction

This month's fiction task is a story in seven postcards, from one person to another. Who is the writer? Who are they writing to? What is the history of their relationship? What is the situation between them now? Jot down some character notes.

The theme is 'wish you were here', so why isn't the person they are writing to with them? Maybe they don't usually go on holiday together, or maybe there has been a falling out, a mix-up over dates, an illness – a death?

Then think about the settings – where is the postcard writer on holiday? What's their accommodation like? Are they with anyone else? Is it unusually quiet, or busy? What's the weather like?

Write a series of seven postcards, one for each day of the holiday. Picture the images on the front before you flip them over and start writing. Can your series of postcards tell the story of the relationship?

'As promised, a picture of the prom! It feels strange being here without you. How's the hip…?', 'I wanted to get you a print but Steffie's so expensive now, I had to settle for this postcard. Who would have thought, all those years ago, that out of the whole class, she'd be the one who would hit the big time…'

Take about twenty minutes.

Non-Fiction

One thing about all the coronavirus lockdowns was that we got to know our own neighbourhoods better, and one thing about the government of the time was that they did love a flag.

Putting these two things together, imagine you are entering a competition to design a flag or emblem for your local village, town, city or area.

Think about objects you might put on your flag. For example, I live in Cornwall and I might put a bucket and crossed spades on mine, an homage to the great Cornish history of piracy as well as representing traditional family holidays on the beach. What should your dominant colour scheme be? Mine is a background of yellow, for sunshine and sand. Make a sketch of your idea.

The competition requires you to describe your flag and explain why it's the perfect representation for your village/town/city/area in less than a hundred words. Take twenty minutes in total.

TIP: Working to a restricted word count usually involves a lot of crossing out and moving things around – it's great practice for writers because it forces us to focus on what's important and make every word count.

Poetry

There's a fabulous poem by former US laureate, Billy Collins, called 'Consolation' – you can find it online – in which he celebrates the pleasures of staying at home and not having to hang around in airports or learn useful phrases in a foreign language. The poem takes on new layers of meaning now, after the experience of national lockdowns.

Write a poem about the benefits of holidaying closer to home. It could be tongue-in-cheek or serious, depending on how you have felt about not being able to travel. If you're going for a rant or being ironic, you could think about using a rhyme scheme – rhyming can be good for comic effect. Take twenty minutes.

AUGUST

Play

The first Wednesday in August is National Playday, a day for celebrating and recognising the importance of play in children's lives. But it isn't only children who need, learn and benefit from playing – all creative work begins with play.

Brenda Ueland, in her book on being a writer, says she soon learnt the best way to approach writing was 'like a child in kindergarten, happily stringing beads'. In this month's free-range writing, see if you can find that feeling, of being completely absorbed in what you are doing just for the pure pleasure of it.

Don't worry about whether what you are writing is good. Let your mind be free to go where it wants – that's always the beginning of the creative adventure. There's only one rule: stick to the timings.

Memoir

Think back to when you were a young child, before the age of about seven. Many people say they have no memory of early childhood, but we aren't looking for whole coherent narratives here, just a few objects and moments.

What was your favourite toy when you were little? If you can remember several, make a list of the first few that come to you. What games did you like to play? Where did you like to play? Jot down some ideas.

Now get a piece of paper, ideally unlined, and an assortment of pens, pencils, felt tips – just whatever you have to hand. Draw a picture of yourself playing, using your non-dominant hand. Take five or ten minutes. Then, still using your non-dominant hand, write a caption. One really good way of feeling like a little child again is drawing and writing with your non-dominant hand.

Reflecting on the process and any emotions or memories that arose for you, write whatever comes, with your normal writing hand, for about five minutes.

Fiction

One of the reasons why writing can be good for wellbeing is because when the pressures of the grown-up world are bearing in on us, creativity lets our inner child rescue us through play. In this story, the protagonist is in some kind of emotional stuck place – perhaps they are stressing about work or grieving over a loss or angry about a situation.

Watching a child playing, or perhaps joining in and playing too, distracts and lifts them out of their perceived problem, enabling them to get a new perspective or sense of proportion, or simply a moment of relief from their grown-up concerns.

Who is your protagonist, and what is the mindset they are stuck in? Who is the child – is it someone they know, or just a stranger they see, at the park maybe, or on TV? Is the child playing alone or with other children? Does the protagonist join in?

How is the protagonist changed by this encounter? What do they learn? How does this moment of pleasure or insight help them to feel better, or inspire them to take action to change their situation?

Write the story. Take twenty minutes.

Non-Fiction

Hide and seek, tag, skipping rhymes, Simon says… games make a great topic for 'how to' articles. I've written a book for children about playground games, drawing on my own childhood and my children's, and various little picture books on things like how to make a feely box.

If you could play a game from your childhood with family or friends, what would it be? French cricket... sardines... shipwrecked...

Write a how-to article describing the game to someone who has never played it. Decide whether you're writing for an adult or child reader – this will give you the content and voice. What equipment will they need? How many people? What's the aim of the game, and have you got any tips on tactics?

Take twenty minutes.

Poetry

Lots of children's traditional rhymes appear to be little pieces of nonsense but can be understood in a serious way by adults, in the same kind of way as lots of jokes and silliness in pantomimes will have adult meanings that would go over a child's head.

Pop goes the weasel – pop is the pawn shop and the weasel is the weasel and stoat, Cockney rhyming slang for coat. It's a silly poem about a serious problem of poverty. Ring o' roses was understood by adults to be about the plague.

Write a children's nonsense poem, that's about some current social or political situation – there are a lot to choose from. Political scandals, the health service, homelessness...

Your poem can be very short or run to several verses and it should rhyme. You might find it helpful to have a nursery rhyme tune in your head to hang it on. Can you imagine actions to go with it?

Take twenty minutes.

Owls

I've had a great fondness for owls ever since a baby one fell into my lap through the open sunroof of my car in a dream many years ago and told me, 'I am your spirit animal for this year!'

So, I am delighted to see that owls have their own special day in August, and what better way for writers to celebrate International Owl Awareness Day than flying free as a bird with a bit of free-range writing? Be wise like the owl – stick to the timings!

Memoir

We automatically associate owls with the words, 'wise, old.' It doesn't necessarily mean old in years, it's just that wisdom is the kind of knowing that comes from life experience rather than through book learning.

Thinking back over your life, who have been your wise owls? Who said something that changed the way you saw things or helped you to do things differently? One of mine might be the American self-help writer, Susan Jeffers, whose book, 'Feel the Fear and Do It Anyway' helped me break through significant hurdles in my earlier life, and my teacher, Jean, whose gentle spirituality showed me a new way of being.

These will be people who may not have been perfectly wise – nobody is perfect – maybe they just had one piece of wisdom for you at a time when you needed to hear it.

Write about your wise owls and what they taught you, whatever comes, for fifteen minutes.

Now, this part might be more difficult: whose wise owl

have you been? Who have you helped with a piece of wisdom of your own, however small? Let go of any misplaced modesty and write for five more minutes.

> TIP: A lot of stories, in real life and fiction, have a mentor figure whose role is to help the protagonist rise to their challenge and provide encouragement, when needed, along the way, whilst not necessarily being directly involved in the action.

Fiction

Most owls are nocturnal – you rarely catch more than a glimpse of them in the headlights and, in the daytime, you don't really see them at all. Your story this month will be about an elusive character, a keeper of secrets, someone that other people confide in, but nobody really knows.

But owls are also raptors, always on the lookout for prey, so putting it all together to create an owl-like character, we have the perfect mix for a blackmailer.

In your story, someone receives a blackmail message from a person they have trusted or never really thought much about in the past. Who is the victim? Who is the blackmailer? What is the relationship between them? Write some notes.

What does the letter say? What does it look like? Write the scene when the victim receives it. What is their first reaction? What do they decide to do? What happens next?

Take twenty minutes.

Non-Fiction

Spend fifteen minutes finding out everything you can about owls. The most enjoyable learning – and therefore the most effective – is when we follow our personal interests, so if you are curious about the anatomy and biology of owls, focus on that. Why do they have the characteristic circle of feathers fanning out around their eyes? Is it true they can turn their heads to almost a complete three-sixty?

If, on the other hand, you are more interested in the symbolism of owls in different cultures, let that be your focus. Owls are not universally associated with wisdom. Take plenty of notes as you go along. Research is a large part of non-fiction writing.

Finish by writing for five minutes about how you found the experience of researching information on owls. How did it feel to discover new facts? How difficult was it? If you had longer, what other things would you like to find out?

Poetry

A friend told me he was walking one afternoon when he suddenly found himself face to face with an owl, sitting on a fence post. The owl didn't move, and for a long moment, they just looked at each other. I wondered which one was the more astonished by the encounter. For my friend, it was an experience of utter mystery and magic.

Write a poem about an encounter between a person and an owl – your non-fiction research will help you to imagine it. Where does this take place? What time of day? Is the owl wild or in captivity? Who is the person – man, woman, child? Write some notes.

Which one of these two – person or owl – will be the 'I' in your poem, or will you take the onlooker point of view? Whichever approach you choose, start by telling the story of the encounter and finish with some kind of comment or reflection. What did it mean to them, how are they changed?

Take twenty minutes.

Holidays

As soon as the school summer holidays start, it feels like everyone's on the move. Airports and motorways are packed with people and the beaches here in Cornwall, where I live, are full of families having fun.

Wherever you are this month, take a holiday from your normal writing with these four free-range writing forays.

Memoir

Aah… those heady childhood summers! They always meant freedom – what else did they mean to you? Take a moment to recall that start-of-the-long-summer-holidays feeling.

Of course, sometimes it could wear off quite quickly, as excitement gave way to boredom. Take a moment to remember that!

How did you used to spend your summer holiday time at home when you weren't away? Who else was there? Who looked after you? What games and activities did you enjoy? Where did you go?

Write about a typical day at home in the summer holidays, from any stage in your childhood.

When one train of thought runs out, go straight on to a typical day from another stage of your childhood. Keep your pen moving on the paper. You aren't trying to create a structured piece of prose, but just to get your memories flowing through writing.

Write for about fifteen minutes.

Now think about summer holiday times away from home. Did you go to different places every year, or did you keep going back to the same ones? What style of holiday did you have – camping or caravanning, self-catering, holiday park, hotel, family visit? Did you ever go on holiday without your family – with your school or youth group, for example?

Write about one holiday you remember well. What were the high points and low points? How did you feel about going? How did you feel about coming home? Ten minutes

Fiction

Someone sees an update from a facebook friend they've never met in real life, asking if anyone would like a free holiday because the person they were planning to go with has had to pull out at the last minute. (Does it sound implausible to you? I heard a news story on the radio this week about someone who did just this!)

They meet for the first time at the airport.

Describe the scene of their meeting. Begin it with your protagonist arriving at the airport to meet his or her travelling companion for the first time and end it with the two of them waiting at the gate to board their plane.

The reader can probably guess from this encounter how well or badly the holiday is likely to go.

Twenty minutes.

Non-Fiction

Write a travel article about a place or attraction you have visited on holiday, focusing on facts and advice for other travellers rather than personal anecdotes.

How did you get there? How much did it cost? What

were the facilities – cafes, toilets, parking and so on? What should other visitors definitely not miss? What was disappointing? Jot down some notes.

What kind of visitor would this place or attraction appeal to – families, seniors, youth groups? Give your piece a title that doesn't just say what it's about, but also who it's for and what's in it for them. For example, 'Family fun for everyone on the English Riviera!' or 'St Ives, an artist's paradise.'

Then get writing! Twenty minutes.

> TIP: You always need to start with a clear idea of who you're writing for. This will affect not just the voice of your piece, but also the content.

Poetry

Imagine finding an object in a charity shop that is clearly a holiday souvenir or, if you happen to be in the High Street, pop into a charity shop and find a real one.

- Who did this souvenir belong to? Picture that person when they first bought and paid for it. How long ago did this happen? Where? What was the weather like on that day?
- What did they do with the souvenir when they got it home?
- Imagine you are that person, and you're holding the souvenir in your hands. How does it feel to be in their clothes? In their shoes?
- How heavy is it? What emotions does it evoke in you? Where do you feel those emotions in your body?

Write a poem, in the first person – 'I' – as the one who bought the souvenir. Address it to the object – 'you.'

Twenty minutes.

Youth

International Youth Day on the 12th of August is a time to highlight the potential of young people in global society and celebrate their achievements. As you'll be harnessing the energy of youth in this month's free-range writing, I probably won't need to remind you to stick to the timings – you've got things to do, places to be, a future to create!

Memoir

Being young is all about looking forward, imagining the kind of person you want to be and the kind of world you want to see. When you were young, what were your dreams for yourself and the world? Who supported your dreams? Who undermined them?

I always wanted to be an artist; my art teachers strongly supported my dream, but my parents blocked it because their priority, coming from very poor backgrounds themselves, was for their children to have careers that were secure and pensionable.

Some people achieve their youthful dreams, but most of us come up against limitations in our circumstances and natural abilities and must adapt or even abandon them. Children who dream of being premier league players might channel the joy of football into playing for a local team in adult life or teaching their own children at the park.

How have your youthful dreams for yourself changed as you've grown older? Have you managed to adapt your ambitions and hold onto the passions that fuelled them? What are your dreams for yourself now? Notice how having future dreams at any stage in life means tapping into the hopeful confidence of youth.

Write the history of the dreams you have had and still have for yourself. Take twenty minutes.

Fiction

In the UK, young footballers like Marcus Rashford are pushing for greater social equality; on the world stage, Greta Thunberg began her campaign for a more sustainable world when she was fifteen. But just as the world needs young people's energy and idealism to fuel change, it also needs the pragmatism and stability of older generations to help effect it.

In this month's story, a young protagonist gets into difficulties at a protest march or demo, and an older person helps them. This older person isn't necessarily on the demo, it could be a police officer or medic, a local resident, a passer-by. Maybe it's a parent or grandparent on the phone.

Make some notes on these two characters, and on the setting. Where is the demo taking place? What do the demonstrators want? It doesn't have to be about climate change or social equality, it could be a local issue or a peace march, for example. How many people are involved? Note the weather and the time of day, the sights, smells and sounds your protagonist will be experiencing in the thick of the action.

Write the story, capturing the passion of the young protester and the strength of their sudden need for assistance set against the calm stability of the older person who helps. Take twenty minutes.

Non-Fiction

Young people need hope for the future because they are the ones who must inhabit it, and up until recently it has felt like a safe bet that life will go on getting better, generation after generation, because that's been the general trajectory since the end of the Second World War. But the pandemic, the climate emergency, the cost-of-living crisis and the conflict on our doorstep in Eastern Europe, are all making it harder to have faith in an ever brighter future.

How can young people feel confident in their ability to forge a good future in an uncertain world? What skills and knowledge might help them? Write an advice piece, as a supportive older person, about how to navigate a good path through life. For inspiration, you could look at Rudyard Kipling's famous poem, 'If.'

Choose your battles, that's a good tip. Look after your health, that's another. If you can't risk failing, you will never succeed. For each instruction, give an example about how you learnt the lesson in your own life. Take twenty minutes.

Poetry

There's an uplifting poem called 'Ode to the Joyful Ones' by Thomas Lux, where he celebrates those people who are always positive and upbeat, whatever difficulties they face. You can find it online. This month's poem is an ode to the young.

Young people are not always idealistic and hopeful. They

feel all their emotions more intensely, their joys, sorrows and despairs, their romances, their rage. Youthfulness is associated with physical strength and energy too.

Celebrate what young people bring to the world, just by being the way they are. If you like, you can use the same repetition of 'Because they bring...' as Lux does in his poem. Take about twenty minutes.

SEPTEMBER

Swap Ideas Day

Here's a good idea: Swap Ideas Day! It falls in September. Sharing ideas that I've found useful or interesting is a big drive for me in my writing, and some of my most enlightening moments have come from other people's books. *Feel the Fear and Do it Anyway*, that was a complete ah-ha for me, courtesy of US author Susan Jeffers, such a simple idea, that it's OK to feel afraid and fear need not stop you doing what you want to do.

I've passed that one on in my children's self-help books along with lots of others, such as the idea that expecting the best or the worst in life is a choice. Think about your own ideas with this month's free-range writing. Perhaps you could pass some on.

Memoir

What is your go-to kind of reading, in different situations? When I'm traveling, I'm not keen on beach reads – I prefer non-fiction that gives me something to ponder as I while away the time. When I'm sad, I like to be distracted by a cosy murder mystery. I have a few favourite blogs I go to for a quick break when I'm working. Write a list, just the first ones that come. If you don't read many books, you could go with music or TV shows instead.

Add specific examples. Carl Greer's *Change Your Story, Change Your Life* got me through a four-hour wait at Manchester airport a few years ago; a batch of Rebecca Tope's Lake District mysteries helped in lockdowns; the Awfully Big Blog Adventure by my friends in the Scattered Authors' Society is always good for a quick read while the kettle's boiling.

Write a piece that goes from the general to the particular, starting with what kind of book/TV/music you enjoy in certain circumstances, then going on to 'One time…' describing a particular occasion and one or two particular books/TV shows/pieces of music. Take twenty minutes. If you finish early, write a second one.

Fiction

Swapping ideas means being willing both to offer your own ideas and listen to other people's but in the modern twitterverse it can be less a swap and more a battle, and political debate is often reduced to 'because it's the right thing to do', with no proper reasoned argument.

In your story, two people have a problem, and they have different ideas about how to solve it. Who? Write some character notes – their name, age and appearance, something about their home life and work or hobbies… just get to know them a bit. What's the relationship between them (if any)?

What's the problem? Maybe they're lost or running late, or they've got a difficult client or a project that isn't going well. Maybe one wants to split up and the other doesn't. Maybe they disagree about someone else's situation, a child struggling at school, an aged parent refusing to accept care.

Can they listen to each other? Can they make the case for their own position? Or is one or both of them confrontational? How do they decide whose idea to go with? How does each of them feel about the decision?

Picture the scene where they discuss the problem, the setting and what they are doing while they talk. The key to writing a passage of dialogue is to remember it's a scene and embed the dialogue in the action. Take twenty minutes.

Non-Fiction

Thinking about one of your skills or hobbies – what helpful tips and hacks could you give a beginner?

As it's a swap, what questions would you ask someone who's got more experience than you?

Write one piece with tips and hacks and one with questions, including examples of times you have felt hampered by not knowing the answers. Take twenty minutes. Notice how writing non-fiction helps you clarify and develop your ideas.

Poetry

In this poem, you'll share your ideas and advice about writing. There are lots of famous poems that do this, so you can find plenty of inspiration online. Some of my favourites are Brian Bilston's 'Ten Rules for Aspiring Poets', because I like its playfulness, 'Introduction to Poetry' by Billy Collins, and 'How to be a Poet' by Wendell Berry.

You'll notice these poems have titles that sound more like non-fiction, and Bilston's is actually laid out as a numbered list. Choose that kind of title for your poem and write some notes on the ideas you would like to share.

The example poems I've given, being by poets, are focused on writing poetry, but your poem could be about any or all kinds of writing. Decide whether you want to include lots of different ideas, like Bilston, or focus on one main idea, like Collins.

Write your poem. Take twenty minutes.

> TIP: This would be a great one to share with your writing group. Write your poems, share what you've written, let everyone benefit from hearing each other's thoughts and advice about writing.

World Peace

The International Day of Peace falls in September. It was initiated by the United Nations General Assembly as an opportunity for everyone around the world to focus on building harmonious relationships, whatever their differences, and celebrate tolerance between nations, individuals and communities.

Peace is not a soft or easy option; it is often hard won and difficult to maintain. That makes it an excellent topic for writing!

So roll up your sleeves and prepare to make peace out of conflict in your free-range writing this month. You know the rule: stick to the timings. Not having time to sit staring at the blank page makes it hard for your inner critic to get a look in.

Memoir

The best peace-making tool in the writer's toolkit is very simple.

Think of a big argument you had with someone. Write the story. Five minutes.

Now imagine you are the other person, and tell the story again, from their point of view. Five minutes.

Finally, imagine you are an onlooker who witnesses the argument. This might be a person you know, a bystander, a fly on the wall…

As the witness, notice everything about the setting and the people involved in the argument – their clothes, facial expressions and body language. Describe the argument, and how you feel about it. Take ten minutes.

In imagination, it's much easier to see the other person's point of view and begin to bridge your differences.

Fiction

My friend Jan once got delayed on her drive home because of a stand-off between two drivers in the middle of a narrow bridge. Neither of them could see why they should be the one who had to pull back, and they'd both made their feelings clear by turning off their engines.

Jan got out of her car to talk to the drivers, one a middle-aged woman and the other, a young man in a suit. Fortunately, she's a counsellor, and she used her counselling skills to persuade one of them to back down.

Think of some conflict situations that might happen between strangers in a public place, such as passengers arguing over a train seat or customers jostling for position in a queue.

Choose one and picture the scene.

Someone intervenes – who? How do they try to calm the situation? What is the outcome of their intervention?

If there are other people in the vicinity, what do they do? This is the mediator's story, so write the scene from their point of view. Take twenty minutes.

> TIP: When you're trying to picture the scene in your story, it can help to imagine you are watching it unfold in a film. From time to time, stop the film and study a still.

Non-Fiction

What do you have definite opinions about? Make a list, just whatever comes. Try to include some not very important things as well as more weighty matters.

For example, what is the right way to eat a cream tea – jam on top or cream on top? That's a no brainer here in Cornwall because the jam sticks satisfyingly to the scone and you can pile on as much cream as you like, but in Devon they have their own reasons for cream first.

Is immigration a good thing, locally, nationally or philosophically speaking? Should students have to pay for their tuition? Is people power going to be effective in tackling the climate emergency?

Write a title, beginning, 'For and against...' For example, 'For and against wearing socks with sandals' or 'For and against open borders in Europe.'

Write the argument from both sides, either in paragraphs or as bullet points. You can explore several different topics or one bigger one in depth. Take a total of twenty minutes.

> TIP: Exploring topics from different angles in non-fiction is a great way of developing your thinking and seeing two sides of an argument.

Poetry

We all have difficult days when we feel out of sorts with our world. At times when you feel lonely, or bored, or confused, or angry, what calms you and brings you a feeling of peace?

I like to walk beside water or go up onto the moor, to

calm my mind when I'm struggling with difficult thoughts and feelings – I find it helps to gaze at wide horizons. You might choose meditation or running, looking through old photos, planning new adventures or having a cup of tea with a friend.

Write a poem, describing a place you go and a thing you do, to get yourself through your difficult days and feel more at peace with your world. Take twenty minutes.

If you need some inspiration, check out Mary Oliver's poem, *Mornings at Blackwater* or Wendell Berry's *The Peace of Wild Things*.

Learning

September is the Festival of Learning Have a Go Month, which celebrates adult learners, tutors and employers who invest in learning projects for their workers. Learning new things can be intensely pleasurable and exciting; it can boost your health, confidence and wellbeing, extend your social life and open up new working opportunities.

Free-range writing helps you learn and develop new writing skills, so what better way to celebrate Have a Go Month than with these free-range writing ideas?

Two rules: stick to the timings... and enjoy! Pleasure is the key to good learning.

Memoir

Think about all the things you have learnt outside formal education and the people who taught you – your grandmother, teaching you how to bake, for example, or your big brother helping you learn to swim. Parents and family members, friends, evening class and workshop leaders – think of all your teachers, how you felt about them and how you feel about them now. What was it that you liked or did not like about their teaching?

Write for ten minutes, whatever comes, not worrying about getting things in chronological order.

When you have finished, think of a skill or subject you would like to learn now. What would learning it give you? Who could help you? What is standing in your way? Write for five minutes.

Imagine yourself three years from now, having acquired that new skill. Look back on the process of learning it and how it has changed your life, from this imagined future. Take five minutes.

Fiction

This story is about someone who is about to go on an adult learning course. Write some character notes: their name, age, something about their appearance.

Why are they taking this particular course, and why at this particular time? What do they hope to get out of it? Write some notes.

Your story begins with them arriving for the very first session and discovering there's someone else on the course that they know and did not want to see. What's the history? Do they both feel the same way about seeing each other again? Does it end in smiles or tears?

Tell the story. Take about twenty minutes.

Non-Fiction

Yoga, cake decorating, dressmaking, dry stone walling, water colour painting, wild food foraging... some of the most popular adult learning classes are not certificated or taught by people with academic or teaching qualifications – they're taught by people with skills they have learnt from experience.

Everyone has things they could teach to others. Jot down some skills you could teach and choose one. Imagine yourself running a workshop, not within the adult education system but as an independent. Where would you choose to run it? I've used art galleries, libraries, Quaker meeting rooms, cafes... all sorts of places including, these days, the virtual space of Zoom.

Picture the people who might come to it. What's the general age range? Mostly men, or mostly women? How does the group look, dress and behave towards each other?

Now you know the place and the kind of person you want to attract, write a flier for your workshop. This must be succinct and include only the most important information, the things that will matter to your target reader. What's the workshop you're proposing? What makes you the right person to teach it? What will the participants get from doing the course? What equipment will they need, and what will be provided?

A very short piece like this will involve a lot of crossing out and rephrasing – the skill is to make it as economical as possible. Play about with it for about twenty minutes.

> TIP: Non-fiction is great practice when it comes to focus and clarity. It makes you identify exactly what you want to say and stick to the point, which is a skill you can bring to all your writing projects.

Poetry

Thinking about the skills you have learnt or would like to learn as an adult, choose one and then google some videos of people practicing that skill. Watch how they move their body and, for a moment, imagine that was you. Imitate the actions so that you can experience what it feels like in your body – for example, if it's yoga, feel the pull of the muscles as you stretch or balance; if it's pottery, the tension in your arms, the resistance of the clay.

Write a poem that begins by simply describing someone practicing this skill, then pull back to yourself as the observer and make any observation you may have about it – what do you think or feel when you watch someone practicing this skill? What does it mean to you?

Take about twenty minutes.

Procrastination

Fight Procrastination Day falls in September, so perhaps you should by making a list of things you've been putting off and start working your way through it. But first, since nothing is that urgent, why not make yourself a nice cup of tea, find a quiet spot and ponder the theme of procrastination with a deliciously diverting bit of free-range writing?

There's only one rule: you know what it is!

Memoir

What did you put off for too long? What were the consequences?

When the first covid lockdown ended, I didn't get to see

some of the people I had really missed because I thought there was no hurry – then the second lockdown came, and I had missed my chance.

Think of examples in your own life of times when you have put things off and missed an opportunity. Try to find some big important ones and some that didn't matter so much. Scan back through the years and find some from different periods in your life.

Choose one to write about. What did you want to do, and why did you hold back? How did it feel when you were putting things off? What was the outcome? What was the lesson? Tell the story. Take twenty minutes.

If you finish early, fill the rest of the time writing about something you are putting off right now. What is holding you back – and could that be a good thing? The consequences of procrastinating are not always bad.

Fiction

'Never do today what you can put off until tomorrow' – that's one of Peony's dad's mottoes in my children's fiction series 'By Peony Pinker.' He's a character whose laziness gets him into all kinds of hot water but also gives him great charm. He cheerfully embraces his flaws. 'If at first you don't succeed, give up!'

Invent a character who always puts things off. Start with their name, age, something about their appearance and a rough idea of their circumstances. Who do they live with? What's their job? What are their hobbies? What do they love, and what do they hate? Are they aware that they always procrastinate? Do they experience it as a problem?

Now invent a second character who certainly does have

a problem with it – in my Peony Pinker stories, that would be Peony's mum. Make some notes on them and their relationship with the first one. What is the last straw for this second character? What makes things come to a head, and what is the outcome? Write the story. Take twenty minutes.

Non-Fiction

Positive procrastination is part of the creative process – it's also known as 'the back burner.' I learnt this early in my career when, after my first book was accepted for publication, I bombarded my agent with new book proposals until she told me to stop and take my time. I seem to recall she used the painful words 'half-baked'.

If you don't give ideas enough time to form up in your mind before you start, the writing process can progress in fits and starts, and involve a lot of sitting staring at a blank page.

Think about the benefits of procrastination. When can it be good to put things off?

Write a defence of procrastination, giving examples to support your argument. You could draw on your own life for examples, such as the time you dithered about putting an offer in on a house you wanted, missed the chance but then found an even better one, or you can use experiences of people you know, such as your neighbour who kept having one more driving lesson because he didn't feel ready to take the test, so got to know the instructor really well and eventually asked them out.

If no real-life examples come to mind, you can always make up some fictional scenarios to illustrate your point. Take twenty minutes.

> TIP: In non-fiction writing, it's important to back up your arguments and ideas with examples and evidence.

Poetry

I used to have a poster on my wall when I was young and frantic that said, 'Things I have to do today: breathe in, breathe out.'

Call your poem, 'Things I have to do today.' You can write as yourself, and the things on your to-do list, or invent a character with their own list of things they have to do and write your poem as them.

Decide on your angle – is your poem going to be humorous, practical, philosophical? Is it going to be short and punchy, long and leisurely, evocative and lyrical? The voice will be related in some way to the things on the list.

Let your poem end with the poet's reflection on what they have to do today. What things do they expect to be able to tick off their list – and how do they feel about that?

Take twenty minutes.

OCTOBER

World Post Day

Dear Reader,

World Post Day is in October and post brings us all kinds of writing, from greetings cards and postcards to personal and business letters, journals and magazines, catalogues and fliers. Free-range writing is also about different kinds of writing and like the post, it can bring surprises.

So, please enjoy this month's postal-themed free-range writing and see what it delivers.

Until next time

Jen

Ps Remember to stick to the timings!

Memoir

What has the postal service meant to you at different times in your life? Take a few moments for a pleasurable ponder.

The first real crush I had was a Swedish boy I met at an international youth camp the summer I was fifteen. We wrote to each other every day till Christmas, funny little letters scrawled on the back of till receipts and toilet paper, scraps of gift wrapping and food packaging. At university, I had a wonderful tutor named Jean, who corresponded with me by post until her death a few years ago although we never met up in person.

The first years of my writing career were characterised by endlessly waiting for the post, for feedback from my agent and proofs from my publishers. These days, personal post comes down to greetings cards rather than letters, and arguments with various public agencies.

Write for twenty minutes, whatever comes, not worrying

about chronological order. Keep your pen moving on the paper even if you're just writing, 'I can't think of a single thing to say…' until something pops into your head. The beauty of flow writing is that it creates a space for ideas to come into, and you never know what ideas might come.

Fiction

The Post Office is one of the last services with the infrastructure to visit every home every day, and there have been trials in various parts of the UK to see if postmen and women could be part of care in the community, keeping an eye on vulnerable people, stopping for a chat and generally checking that everything is OK.

This story takes the form of the 'magic three' – something happens; the second time it happens, that sets the pattern, but the third time breaks it. Lots of children's stories take this form. 'This porridge is too hot, so she leaves it… this porridge is too cold, so she leaves it… this porridge is just right, and she gobbles it up.'

Your postman or postwoman is on their round, and maybe they stop at a particular house to chat, or maybe they go straight past, or maybe they have to dodge the dog; the next day, the same thing happens again, but on the third occasion, something is different. Instead of getting on with their round, they pause. What happens next?

As always, you need to know your protagonist (your main character) – what is your postman or postwoman like? How do they feel about their job? What kind of mood are they in today? Write notes until you get a good sense of them. Then write the story. Take twenty minutes.

Non-Fiction

Do we still need letter post? Could all official communications and personal messages come via email these days or are there still times when a letter is better? I personally don't care for email invitations and greetings cards, and I rarely watch video greetings all the way through – I skip to the message.

When ebooks were invented, people said it would be the death of paperbacks, but that hasn't happened so far. Could the internet herald the end of physical cards and letters? Write an opinion piece. Take twenty minutes.

Poetry

An epistolary poem is a letter in the form of a poem. The title or first line often begins 'Dear...' You can find lots of great examples online such as 'Dear David' by Matthew Burgess.

Your poem could be a personal letter to a friend or family member – remember they don't have to be real people, you're 'the poet' and 'the poet' doesn't necessarily have to be yourself. It could be a formal letter, such as explaining to the Inland Revenue why you are not going to pay the 19p you owe them however many final demands they send. It could be to the Readers' Letters page of a magazine, a personal invitation, a thank you or a message of condolence.

Start by writing your letter in prose, to get the voice and tone, then cut, build and shape it into a poem, keeping it free unless it wants to slip into a regular meter and rhyme. Take five minutes for the prose preparation and fifteen for the poem.

Older People

The coronavirus pandemic made many of us feel more aware of how vulnerable the older people in our lives can be, and how important. The International Day of Older Persons, on October 1st, is an opportunity to celebrate and appreciate older people everywhere, and to think about the social contribution they make.

So this month's free-range writing is all about celebrating older people, including the older person you hope to become.

Memoir

One of the things you realise as soon as you start writing memoir is that there are lots of gaps in the information you hold about the past.

Thinking about a parent or grandparent, jot down some notes about their life – their date of birth and other significant dates, places they have lived, jobs they have done, their family circumstances.

Try to write their story, noting down the gaps, whenever you come across something you don't know. Take twenty minutes. If you run out of things to say before the time is up, try telling the story of a different parent or grandparent.

If the person is still alive, ask them to fill in the gaps – if they aren't, ask someone else who might know. One of the pleasures of writing memoir is that it's an opportunity to find and fill in the gaps.

Fiction

In many stories, there is a mentor figure who helps the protagonist to accept and engage with the challenge he faces. The mentor could be anyone who has wisdom and knowledge that the hero has not yet acquired for himself, so older people commonly fill this role.

My own children's stories have featured two wise old next door neighbours, Mr Kaminsky in the *Peony Pinker* series, and Miss Fischer in *Miss Fischer's Jewels*; a wise and wily great aunt, in *Looking After Auntie,* and several lovely loving grandmothers, who help and advise my young protagonists.

In your story, someone is worried about showing their true colours – maybe they want to make a declaration of love or come out to their parents or admit to a mistake. Make some character notes – their name, age, appearance. What makes them feel happy, what makes them feel annoyed? What are they worried about revealing? Who do they want – or not want – to reveal it to?

Now create a mentor figure, an older person who cares about them and has the life experience to be able to encourage and support them. Write some character notes.

This story is the little scene in which the mentor helps the protagonist to make the decision that they will take a chance and reveal their truth. The decision is the end of the scene – don't go on to tell what happens next. Take fifteen minutes.

> TIP: The role of mentors in fiction is about encouraging and advising the protagonist to take action; they don't usually take part in the action themselves. The mentor doesn't have to be older than the protagonist, but older people often play the mentor role, in fiction as in life.

Non-Fiction

Jenny Joseph's famous poem, 'Warning', begins with the lines, 'When I am an old woman I shall wear purple/With a red hat which doesn't go, and doesn't suit me...' and goes on to list all the outrageous things the poet plans to do 'to make up for the sobriety of my youth'.

For this month's non-fiction, write your own manifesto for aging, beginning, 'When I am old, I will...' In older age, we have fewer work and family responsibilities and more time, and we may feel far less worried about what other people think of us. What uses will you make of those greater freedoms? Take twenty minutes.

Imagining the future you want creates a space you can move into, insofar that you cannot achieve something that you have not first been able to imagine yourself achieving – so this isn't just a non-fiction writing exercise, it's a practical first step to getting the future you want.

Poetry

Picture an elderly person in their home – this could be real or fictional. Notice the colours, styles, details in the environment they have created for themselves, and the objects they like to have around them.

Write a poem that gives a sense of who they are and possibly some of their history from elements in their home environment, beginning, 'It is...' It is the silver biscuit barrel on the oak sideboard/ The cleaner comes to polish every week/ It is the Radio Times folded open on tomorrow's date/ Crossed with reading glasses and a ballpoint pen...'

You could make this a list or focus in on just one or

two objects in greater detail, repeating the prompt, 'It is...' as often as you like. Take twenty minutes.

Libraries

8-13th October is National Libraries Week. Many people assume that libraries and physical books in general are doomed but, according to the Libraries Week website, more visits are made to public libraries in Great Britain every year than to all cinemas, theatres, live music gigs and the UK's top ten tourist attractions put together.

Anyone can go into any public library and libraries, like cafes, can be wonderful places to write. Wherever you happen to be, at home or on your travels, pop into a library and try it for yourself with some of this month's free-range writing. But even when you're out and about, remember to stick to the timings.

Memoir

What is the history of libraries in your life? Did you have a school library, where you went to read, or a university library where you studied for exams? Did you use your public library as a child, or at any other stage in your life? I personally didn't know there was such a thing as a public library until I got a job in one after I graduated.

Perhaps you have used or visited workplace or private libraries? Write a list of all the libraries you remember visiting. Choose three, and write for five minutes about each, describing both the library building and environment and your experience of being there. What kind of books did you take out? What did having that resource mean to you?

If you have never used a library, visit your local one. Have a good look round, then go home and write about the experience for twenty minutes. Memoir doesn't have to be about the distant past; you can write memoir about something you did five minutes ago.

Fiction

Two people meet in a library, in what will prove to be the start of an unlikely friendship.

Jot down some ideas. For example, someone might help a stranger with using the computer, or read to a fractious toddler while his mother chooses her books or recommend a book they have enjoyed.

Decide on the scenario, then write some notes on the two main characters involved.

The scope of the story is just this initial meeting in the library. There isn't room in a short story to give all the background and future developments, so think of it as a 'glimpse and insight' – two lives suggested in that moment of meeting, and a sense of how things will develop.

Take about five minutes for the character notes and fifteen for the story.

> TIP: It can be hard to imagine stories in unfamiliar settings so, if you never use public libraries, this could be a good time to pay a visit.

Non-Fiction

Write an opinion piece about public libraries. The title should express your view – for example, 'Why we don't need public libraries any more' or 'Cutting funding for libraries is short-sighted and wrong.'

Give three or four reasons why you feel the way you do, and back up your arguments with evidence and examples.

Take about twenty minutes.

> TIP: Non-fiction can be fuelled by emotion, just the same as fiction. If wasting money on libraries or depriving young and disadvantaged people by cutting library services makes you angry, use that anger to help you express your case more strongly.

Poetry

Public libraries make books accessible to everyone, no matter how poor they are, and books are a vital source of pleasure, information and insights into our own and other people's life experiences.

Write a list of books you've loved or hated at different times in your life. Choose one. Where were you when you read this book?

The first one that comes to mind as I'm writing this is *Writers Dreaming*, by Naomi Epel, which I started reading on the train to London and found so fascinating I abandoned my sightseeing plans, found a quiet square and sat down to read for the rest of the day.

My second one is *The Wishing Chair Again*, by Enid Blyton, which takes me right back to being six years old, curled up in a huge armchair.

Close your eyes and think yourself back to the time and place when you read the book you've chosen. Use all your senses to fully remember it. Notice what you can see around you, what you can hear, the smell of the air.

Look down at the book in your hands. What does it look like, feel like, smell like? What emotions do you feel as you open it – what is its promise?

Write a poem about the experience of reading this book. What did it mean to you – and what might it mean to your reader?

Take about twenty minutes.

Drawing

The Big Draw goes on throughout the month of October. It's the world's largest drawing festival with events taking place in museums, schools, galleries and community centres, the goal being to promote visual literacy and art education.

Visual awareness is important for creative writers in lots of ways, so drawing is a great theme to explore in free-range writing. I always say there's just one rule – stick to the timings. But this is writing you do purely for yourself, so the other rule is, enjoy it!

Memoir

In my creative journaling courses, I encourage people to include drawings, sketches and collages and play about with shapes and colours in the way they organise their text. Besides being fun, it frees up your thinking.

If today was a colour, what would it be? First answer, jot it down. Take that colour and write about it for three minutes, just whatever comes, not trying to link it to your day at all. Just playing.

Write the history of that colour in your life. Take about five minutes. Orange was a favourite for me, and once in a street auction when I made the winning bid, I remember the trader shouting, 'Sold to Miriam in the norange!' Why did he give me the name 'Miriam', and why did he say 'norange' instead of 'orange'? Was that what made it memorable to me? In later years I went right off orange and switched my allegiance to blues and greens. Now I like it again, but I wouldn't wear it.

Make some kind of visual image. If you have a pritt stick to hand and a few old brochures or magazines in the recycling, tear bits out and make a collage that is mostly that colour. You can include odd words or details that aren't the same colour but seem to fit.

If you have coloured pencils, you could make a drawing instead, mostly in that colour. If you've only got the pen you're writing with, draw a picture of objects you associate with your colour and use your imagination. Take as long as you like.

Finish by writing for about three minutes about the process of creating the image – how did it feel? Did it spark any new thoughts or ideas?

Fiction

The setting for this story is a life drawing class, where a naked model is sitting for a group of artists. What is the situation – art school, evening class, artist's studio? How does the model feel in their body? Use all your senses to imagine the warmth or coolness of the air on their skin, the touch of the floor or chair they are sitting, standing or lying down on. Who is in the group? How does the model feel emotionally about sitting for them?

There is a person in the group that the sitter knows but did not expect to see in this situation. What is the history between them? How do they know each other? How does the model feel about this person seeing them naked? How does the artist feel?

Write two monologues about the experience, one by the model and one by the group participant. Start with the moment they first saw each other in this unexpected way, and end with what has changed for each of them by the end of the session. Take ten minutes for each piece.

Non-Fiction

Make some kind of visual image – a still life of objects in your home, a sketch of houses in your street, a portrait of your own face in the mirror... whatever you fancy. The important thing is to take your time. Spend at least ten minutes.

Write a recount of that experience. How did you feel before you began? Did you experience some resistance? What thoughts and feelings arose when you were making art? What changes did you notice in your body? What do you feel about the image that you made? Could there be benefits for all of us in making art, purely for pleasure? Take ten minutes.

Poetry

A poem is a visual object – one of the things that makes it a poem is it looks like a poem on the page, with white space all around it. This poem will be about something you can draw in outline, such as a mug of coffee or a shoe.

Sketch its shape and make a poem that fits inside it. If you need inspiration, search 'shape poems' and you'll find lots of examples online. Then write a poem about your object that has a more formal shape – couplets of the same length, for example, or four-line stanzas with a closing couplet.

Experiment with different forms for the same subject, perhaps long and rambling free, or short and compact like the poems William Carlos Williams wrote on the back of his prescription pad between patients.

Notice how changing the shape of your poem affects the mood and content of the writing.

NOVEMBER

Bonfire Night

Bonfire Night is keenly anticipated by many families and dreaded by many pet owners. Love it or loathe it, it's a great topic for writing across different genres, so let your creativity sparkle with this month's free-range writing.

Memoir

Most people have memories of bonfire nights throughout their life, from a few Catherine wheels and rockets in the back garden to parties with friends and big organised fireworks displays. I remember, in my childhood, boys on street corners with their guys on go-karts, shouting out, 'Penny for the guy!' I remember being afraid that the sparklers would burn through my mittens and, scrolling forwards, I remember my children's excited faces as I lit the sparklers in their little gloved hands.

Write about your memories of bonfire night, just whatever comes, for fifteen minutes. Start 'I remember…' and repeat the prompt as often as you like. Don't worry about trying to stick to chronological order. Free writing like this is a way of creating space to let your mind go wherever it wants to, and that is a necessary skill for writers.

After fifteen minutes, write for another five, reflecting on your memories and how you think and feel about bonfire night now.

> TIP: If you didn't grow up in the UK, adapt this exercise to your experiences of fire festivals in the culture you grew up in.

Fiction

It's a bonfire party, a dark November night, with a group of family and/or friends. Where is it taking place? Who is hosting it? What is the weather like? Picture the setting. Picture the people, all wrapped up against the cold. Use your senses – hear the sounds of the party, notice the smells in the air. Jot down some notes.

Between fireworks, the place is plunged into darkness. When the faces are all lit up, the point-of-view character is not looking at the firework, but at the people around them. They catch sight of someone they thought they knew well and have a sudden moment of insight. For example, it could be that this person is having an affair, or feeling worried about something ... they could be dangerous, or in danger...

Does the person realise they are being watched? Is there any eye contact? What happens next?

Tell the story in the first person – 'I' – from the point of view of the one who has the insight. Take twenty minutes.

Non-Fiction

Guy Fawkes tried to blow up the House of Lords. When? Why? And who was Guy Fawkes? This month's non-fiction task is a fact-finding mission.

I seem to have managed to get through quite a long life with only the sketchiest idea of what Guy Fawkes' Night was all about until I did a bit of googling to research this article. Did you know, Guy Fawkes fell from the scaffold and broke his neck, so sparing himself the agony of being hanged, drawn and quartered?

When you have all the info, either tell the story or write

a numbered list of fascinating facts about the life and death of Guy Fawkes. Take fifteen minutes.

> TIP: Writing non-fiction is good practice for writers of every stripe because it starts with a body of research material that you have to distil down to the most important points. In non-fiction, as in fiction and memoir, the finished piece is like the tip of the iceberg. There is always a much larger mass of material hidden beneath.

Poetry

This month's poetry task is a narrative poem – a poem that tells a story – and you can choose one of the stories from any of these bonfire night tasks: an incident you recalled in memoir, the fictional anecdote you wrote where somebody has a sudden insight at a bonfire party or the true story of Guy Fawkes that you researched for your non-fiction.

Narrative poems are often longer and follow a pattern of rhythm and rhyme – think folk songs and nursery rhymes. 'Remember, remember the fifth of November/Gunpowder, treason and plot/ I see no reason why gunpowder treason should ever be forgot…'

If you fancy giving rhyming verse a go, check out a few narrative poems first to get in the mood, or listen to some traditional folk songs. 'The Lady of Shallott' by Alfred Lord Tennyson has a very clear structure, beginning with a description of the setting, then the character, then the action – the lady's temptation and what happens next.

A narrative poem needs all the same elements as a prose

story, so think about settings, characters and plot. Take twenty minutes.

NaNoWriMo

For writers, November can only mean one thing – NaNoWriMo. It's nearly twenty years since November became National Novel Writing Month, and now hundreds of thousands of people take part every year.

Lots of people say they would write a novel if they had time and NaNoWriMo is an opportunity to make time, by dedicating yourself to writing 50,000 words in 30 days. That's less than 2.000 words per day – tough but do-able. At the very least, by the end of it, participants will know how it feels to write a novel, and some will come away with a first draft that feels worth working on.

So this month's free-range forays are all about writing novels.

Memoir

Most writers seem to regard literary fiction as the pinnacle of a writing career, and everything else just a step on the ladder. It's almost as if you can only consider yourself a proper writer when you have written a novel.

This makes as much sense as thinking you can only consider yourself a proper runner when you have run a marathon. Some runners are sprinters.

Some writers are not naturally novelists, but almost every writer has thought about writing a novel. Have you? What would it be about? If you've thought about writing more than one novel, what would they all be about?

I wrote my first novel when I was seventeen and went on to write several murder mysteries and literary novels before I decided I didn't really enjoy living in fictional worlds for such extended periods of time. But I did like writing fiction, so I followed my agent's advice and tried children's fiction, which although it isn't easier, is usually much shorter.

Write the history of novel writing in your life, all your plans and projects, right up to how you feel about it now and what you hope for in the future. Take about twenty minutes.

Fiction

When you're writing a novel it can be easy to literally lose the plot and find yourself floundering, with no idea which way to go. The problem is almost always that you've lost the focus on the main protagonist and what he or she wants, which is the driving force in every story.

You can use this simple interview technique to create a protagonist you care about and reconnect with them any time your plot is starting to drift.

First find a character by flicking through a magazine or searching online for a photo of someone who sparks your interest. Only take a few minutes – everyone is interesting.

Look closely at the photo, and then write for two minutes, describing their physical appearance.

Now ask them these questions and jot down their answers, in their own voice.

- What's your name? How old are you?
- Where do you live? How long have you lived there?
- What is your work, or what was your work before you retired?

- Who are the most important people in your life?
- If your house was on fire, what would you rescue?
- How do you feel about Christmas?

Supposing you could interview them at greater length – where would you suggest meeting? What would you like to ask? Close your eyes and imagine this meeting. Use all your senses to fully be there. Notice what your character is wearing, their body language, the tone of their voice. Write the scene. Take ten minutes.

> **NOTE**: If you meet up with your protagonist several times in this way, think of these meetings as simply a chance to get to know them better, outside the world of the story.

Non-Fiction

Non-fiction usually includes research or at least some checking of facts. NaNoWriMo is an online project, so go to their website and find out exactly how it works. Jot down anything that feels particularly interesting to you.

Then write an opinion piece, with a title such as *Why I would never do NaNoWriMo* or *How NaNoWriMo could help your writing*.

If you don't have strong opinions, write a fact file instead, such as *Everything you need to know about NaNoWriMo*.

Take twenty minutes.

Poetry

Imagine you're a person who has written poems, short stories or non-fiction articles but never a novel, and you don't feel like a proper writer. The kind of person who, when asked if they've done much writing, will say 'No, not really. Only poetry,' or 'Just short stories.'

As that person, write a humorous poem about your writing life, listing all your excuses about why you haven't got around to writing a novel yet. Take twenty minutes.

Stress

National Stress Awareness Day falls in November. According to the Mental Health Foundation, three quarters of UK adults have felt under so much mental or emotional pressure in the last year that they have found it difficult to cope, and that doesn't seem surprising when our personal issues are playing out against a backdrop of global problems such as wars, pandemics and climate change.

Writing is a great way to de-stress because it is what psychologists call a 'flow activity' – when we're writing, we get caught up in it and stop thinking about anything else. So, take a break from the stresses and strains with this month's free-range writing.

Memoir

What do you worry about? Jot down your current top three worries. For example, my job, my health, the political situation. Add some detail – My job: what if there's another round of redundancies, what if I miss my deadline... Health: eyesight, shoulder pain...

Now, thinking back, what did you worry about at points in the past? When I was a little girl, I was terrified I would never get to be a grown-up because London would be wiped out by a nuclear bomb, and we'd all be turned to vapour. As a teenager, I worried that my father would have another heart attack and die. Jot down the first five examples you think of, from different times in your life.

Focusing on one of these past worries, what helped? Who helped? How did it turn out? Tell the story for five minutes.

What strategies have you developed over the years for handling stress? For me, walking, writing and, during the coronavirus lockdowns, knitting (with mixed success). What strategies might you consider trying in the future? I might try to grow vegetables. Write about your go-to strategies for about five minutes, just whatever comes.

Finally, focus on one of those strategies and write a message of gratitude to it. 'Dear daily walk…' How do you feel when you are walking, writing or whatever? What does it give you? Take five minutes.

Fiction

Imagine you are watching a film. It's a scene where the main character is feeling extremely stressed – maybe they are in physical danger, or under emotional pressure from a relationship, or overwhelmed by the demands of their current situation. What is causing them such stress? How long has it been going on?

Freeze frame and examine their body language and the tension in their face – copy that in your own face and body, to help you imagine how they are feeling.

Now start the film again and watch the scene play out. Something happens that pushes them over the edge – it might be something very small. That is the nature of last straws. What is it? Who else is involved? Does the main character lash out, or do something rash, or break down?

Tell the story of how things became so tense, ending with the moment when the tension comes to a head and is broken by the main character's sudden reaction. Take about twenty minutes.

Non-Fiction

Write a guided meditation for stress – if you don't know what that is, you can find lots of examples on youtube.

Start with instructions to your listener on how to settle their body and prepare for the visualisation – this may include sitting or lying down, depending on whether it's a five-minute refresher or a half hour sleep meditation, closing or lowering the eyes and focusing on the breathing – test your suggestions on yourself and decide what is the best preparation.

Then tell your listener to imagine being in a beautiful calm environment – perhaps a garden, or a beach, or beside a woodland stream. Wherever you choose, describe it using all the senses, so your listener can fully imagine being there.

As you write, notice the effects on your own body – is imagining this for your listener having a calming effect on you?

When you have finished, take a few slow breaths yourself and then read your piece aloud, feeling the slow rhythm of the words. Take a total of about twenty minutes.

Poetry

Stress is all about being in your head, worrying about an imagined future and generally over-thinking. You can bring your focus back down to earth by simply noticing your physical environment and the objects within it.

Looking around you, choose any object, however

unpoetic it might seem. Look at it from every angle, touch it with your fingers. If it isn't too big, pick it up and feel its weight. Does it have a smell? Does it make a sound? What would it say to you right now if it could talk? What would you say to it? Write a poem to this object, starting 'You…'

Keep it free verse, not locking it into a fixed rhyming scheme, but enjoying the musicality of the words you use, their sounds and natural rhythms. Take twenty minutes. In writing a poem you are creating another object that will calm you as you pay attention to it.

Road Safety

Free-range writing is personal writing. The fact that no one else is going to read it means you can experiment and play, and the fact that the pieces are timed means your inner critic doesn't have a chance to get in the way.

Using personal writing to explore aspects of everyday life that you may never have given much thought to is a great way to find fresh ideas and inspiration from your own experience, and trying different genres is a real creative work-out.

This month's theme is road safety, which has its very own national week in November. So, ponder, be playful – and stick to the timings.

Memoir

Everyone has had experiences relating to road safety, even if they haven't personally been involved in an accident. Maybe a close family member or friend has crashed their car, or had a near-miss, like my mother who passed out at the wheel in her late eighties, or my daughter, whose puppy was run over by a cyclist a few months ago.

Jot down some ideas and when you have several, choose one.

Remember memoir is stories, like fiction. Think about settings – where did this take place? What time of day; what time of year? How was the weather? Were there lots of people around? Who was directly involved? Think about dialogue – you don't need to be able to remember exactly what people said, or even to have been present, to use dialogue as part of a story.

Just as with writing fiction, try to make sure your story has an intriguing beginning, a middle that involves action and a satisfying ending. Take twenty minutes.

> TIP: If the accident happened to someone else and you weren't there, yours will be a story within a story, both what happened in the accident and also the story of how you heard about it and did or did not get involved, and you will want to apply the questions and think about the structure in connection to both.

Fiction

This month's fiction stretches the topic to include a different kind of road safety, where the car feels like a safe space to raise a difficult subject because there isn't any opportunity for eye contact, rather like in the religious confessional. Difficult conversations in the car can also lead to actual road safety issues, and your story might or might not take that direction too.

Who is the driver? Make some character notes. Who is the passenger, and what is the relationship between them? More notes. Which of them needs to have this conversation? How does the other one respond? How is the situation between them changed between the beginning and end of the conversation?

This is an opportunity to write a dialogue-heavy scene, so try to imagine the way each character speaks, their tone of voice and mannerisms. Write the story. Take twenty minutes.

Non-Fiction

I live on a narrow lane opposite a rural school and parents parking opposite to drop off their children used to obstruct passing traffic, sometimes resulting in damage to other parked cars and presenting a danger to children because of blocked visibility. So local residents wrote to the parish council and community police and a no-stop zone was established in front of the school.

Some years later, speed bumps were placed on the main road in such a way that drivers were forced onto the wrong side of the road where there was no visibility due to a dip ahead. Residents wrote letters; the speed bumps were re-located.

In the form of an email or letter to a local paper/website/magazine, write about a road safety issue in your area. Identify the problem and suggest some practical actions that could be taken to resolve it, giving your reasons. Take twenty minutes.

> TIP: Writing about real life situations in non-fiction can spark ideas for stories and poems. Just ask, 'What if?' What if a driver didn't see a child walking out between parked cars outside your local school, or misjudged the width of the gap and damaged another vehicle? You already have the settings and the situation – your imagination will do the rest.

Poetry

There are some flowers on lamp post or tied to a broken bollard or laid on a grassy verge, where someone has lost their life in a road accident. Picture the scene. Is it a suburban street, or a busy bypass, or a country lane?

Are there lots of flowers, or just a single offering? What kind of flowers are they, and are they fresh or wilted or completely dead? Are there other objects around the flowers that might give some clues as to what happened? A note with a name, cards and messages, a children's toy, a woman's necklace…

The movement of your poem is from a straightforward description of the flowers using all your senses to a personal reflection on your thoughts or feelings as you look upon them. Take twenty minutes.

DECEMBER

Handmade Gifts

In the run-up to Christmas, many of us start thinking about what presents we might give or receive. National Make a Gift Day, on the third of December, is a reminder that we don't necessarily have to spend a fortune in order to give something unique and personal.

A handmade gift always feels special, from the picture of you that your grandchild painted to the hanging flower basket your partner put together or the photo collage your friend made for your birthday.

Making presents instead of buying them is also much more eco-friendly, especially if they are either consumables, such as sloe gin, jam or biscuits, or made from recycled materials. So if you or the people you want to give presents to are concerned about the climate emergency, this could be a good year to consider whether you might make instead of buy.

Explore your thoughts and feelings about handmade presents with these free-range writing ideas. Writing across different genres is a great creative work-out anyway, and these might also spark some new seasonal gift ideas.

Memoir

Have you ever received a handmade gift? This might be something as simple as a card or home-made cake, or a real labour of love, such as a hand knitted sweater. Make a list.

Have you ever given someone a gift you made yourself? Make another list.

Have you ever watched someone receive a handmade gift from someone else, and either wished they had made that gift for you or felt relieved that they hadn't?

Make some notes about the emotional quality of these experiences. When you received each of the handmade gifts in your first list, did you feel delighted, embarrassed, blessed, burdened? When you gave each of the handmade gifts in your second, how did that feel, and how did you think it was received?

Take your time – about ten minutes for this part of the task.

Choose one gift from one of your lists. Write the story of how, when, where and why it was made and given. Take ten minutes.

Fiction

Gifts are part of all sorts of social celebrations, including birthdays, weddings, retirements and housewarmings, but sometimes they don't require a special occasion at all. We may use gifts to express all sorts of things – love, forgiveness, sympathy, apology and gratitude, to name a few.

In this story, someone receives a handmade gift, and doesn't like it. Do they try to disguise their feelings? Do they succeed? Or are they quite open about how they feel?

Make some character notes – who is receiving the gift, and who has made it for them?

Now some notes on the situation. What is the relationship history between these two? Why this particular gift, and why now?

Finally, write some notes on the setting. Where and when (time of day, time of year) is the gift giving taking place?

Write the scene. End with a detail that gives the reader a glimpse of how the relationship may be changed by this gift giving. Take fifteen minutes.

Non-Fiction

For your non-fiction writing, choose one of these tasks:

- An article based on a numbered list – these may be a mix of different kinds of handmade presents or all on the same theme, such as things you can knit, cook or paint.
- A how-to article, giving step by step instructions on how to make one specific handmade gift.

As usual, think about who you are writing for. This task could be a nice one to write for children, depending on what skills the gift-making requires. Start by jotting down some ideas, then take about fifteen minutes to craft your article.

If the whole idea of giving or receiving handmade presents fills you with horror, try making your article humorous.

Poetry

Think of this poem as a hand-crafted gift. Who would you like to make it for? What would you like to say to them?

Start by writing in prose, just whatever comes, beginning' 'Dear…' and their name. Don't overthink it – this is just a warm-up, to get you in the zone. Keep your pen moving on the paper for three minutes. Then pause. Consider what it is that you haven't said. Write on, for a further three minutes.

Read back over what you have written and underline a few words or phrases you might like to include in your poem.

Take about fifteen minutes to write your poem. Decide whether to keep it free or follow a regular rhythm or and rhyming scheme, depending upon what you feel the person you are writing for would prefer.

If you're happy with it, why not pop it in an envelope and send it to them?

Elf Day

With a nod to Christmas, Elf Day in December is a fun and colourful way for the Alzheimer's Society to raise funds and awareness. Dementia is a topic that touches most of us, either because we know or care for someone who has it, or simply because it will affect so many of us in our lives that we may worry when we can't remember a word or forget what we went upstairs for.

Writing on a single theme across different genres enables us to engage on every level, body, mind, heart and soul, to arrive at a deeper awareness, provide material we might work up into a finished piece and also develop our writing style. Give it a go with this month's dementia-themed free-range writing.

Non-Fiction

We don't usually start with non-fiction, but it will be helpful for your stories and poems if you have done some research first. Alzheimer's is a form of dementia. The facts and figures are interesting, but your main focus will be living with dementia and if you put that in a search engine you will find lots of information about the day-to-day effects on sufferers and carers at different stages of the disease.

If you know someone who is living with dementia themselves or caring for someone with the condition, they will be able to offer more personal insights, so why not give them a call? Writing about real life can be a great opener for interesting conversations.

This task is purely research which is the first stage of non-fiction writing. You will need the full twenty minutes just for reading articles and making notes. Notice, when you go on to the other genres, how having information on your theme fresh in your mind makes it easier to develop your stories and poems.

Memoir

Write for ten minutes about your personal experience, thoughts, feelings and fears around dementia, whatever comes. Don't try to structure it; just let it go where it wants to. When one line of thought runs out, simply start another.

When simply start writing and keep your pen moving on the paper, something always comes, and what comes might surprise you.

When the time is up, read back over what you have written and underline any words or sentences that jump out at you.

Then write a reflection on the whole experience. What did the flow writing feel like? What did you discover about yourself and the topic of dementia? Take five minutes. If you'd like to try something different, you could do this part in the third person, instead of 'I'. 'When she started writing, she thought…' Playfulness and experimentation is the root of creativity.

Fiction

I run a lot of writing workshops, so I hear a lot of stories, and one that has stayed with me was by someone describing a trip to her local shop with her husband who had Alzheimer's. She didn't think anyone would be interested to hear it, because it felt to her like just a humdrum part of a humdrum life, but for people who have imagined dementia without experiencing it her story was riveting, and for those who had cared for a dementia-sufferer, it was affirming. Through small moments and details, she brought the situation vividly to life.

This fiction piece is a scene between a dementia-sufferer and their carer, who may or may not be a family member. Write some character notes about each. How much does the dementia affect their day-to-day life? What are their hopes and fears for the future? Their feelings about the past? What is their living situation? What is the history between them?

The story I've described began with the couple entering the shop and ended when they left. Your story is likely to feel small too, in terms of action. The trick with this one is to really feel your way into the characters and capture the moment as vividly as possible. Take twenty minutes.

Poetry

People who are suffering from memory loss often make lists. For this month's poetry task, imagine you are in the early stages of dementia, beginning to forget important things, and write a list poem.

A list poem is just what it sounds like, a list of things, people, places or thoughts. What makes it a poem is the language and musicality, perhaps including repetitions, the organisation of your material, and the movement towards a satisfying closing line or couplet.

What kind of things might your list include? How can you make it clear the narrator is suffering from dementia?

For example, in a list titled 'Telephone numbers', the narrator might include names and roles in brackets – Jim Farley (plumber), Archway Stores (newspapers) and so on, and end with Rachel (daughter).

Try a couple of different ideas. Take twenty minutes.

Volunteering

December is a time for giving and International Volunteer Day, on the fifth, is an opportunity to recognise and celebrate the contribution of people who give the most precious gift of all, the gift of their time.

Almost everyone will have volunteered for something at some point, and we will certainly all have benefited from the work of volunteers, although their work can often go unnoticed. Writing is a way of noticing the things we take for granted, so let's recognise the wonderful work of volunteers with this month's free-range writing.

Memoir

When did you benefit from the work of volunteers? Think of instances from the distant past, such as Cub Scouts or Brownies, right up to the present day. A long time ago, I took my children to volunteer-run playgroups and events run by school PTA's. These days, I belong to several writing organisations that are run by volunteer committees. I often have a browse in charity shops and, recently, I've noticed a family picking up litter in my neighbourhood to keep it nice for everyone. Jot down some ideas.

Do you remember any particular people whose volunteer work made a difference? For a while, one of our playgroup organisers was a much older woman named Margaret, who was more like a grandmother to the children and a mother figure for the mums.

Write for ten minutes, just whatever comes, about the voluntary organisations and individual volunteers whose work has enriched your life.

When did you volunteer yourself? Maybe you helped to organise an event, or manned a stall, or did some shopping for a neighbour, or sat on a committee. For some people, that will be a long list – for others, like me, it could be disappointingly short. Write for ten minutes about your own experience of volunteering, including any future aspirations.

Fiction

Somebody is mean to a volunteer – maybe they are critical or angry. The volunteer reacts in a surprising way, perhaps retaliating, walking out, or bursting into tears. For example, I once played in a darts team for our local pub and at the annual general meeting someone questioned the treasurer on her record keeping, suggesting there should be more money in the bank account. To everyone's astonishment, the treasurer stood up and threw her drink over her.

Both the accuser and the treasurer felt bad about the incident and in your story, both the mean person and the volunteer feel bad too. Where does this encounter take place? Who else is there? Write the story from the point of view of an onlooker, in the first person, 'I'. What do you think about what's going on? Do you get involved? How is the situation resolved?

Take twenty minutes.

Non-Fiction

Do you know someone who has done voluntary work? Several of my friends have worked in charity shops; one, who used to be a library manager, worked behind the scenes, valuing second-hand books for a charity's online shop. My daughter walks dogs for people who can't give their pets enough exercise, through www.borrowmydoggy.com. Maybe you have a friend who has served on a committee, or helped with a one-off fundraiser?

Interview them about their experience, either in person or on the phone or using social messaging. Ask them exactly what the work entailed, and why and how they got involved. How did they find the experience of volunteering – what were the highs and lows? If they don't still volunteer, why did they stop? Would they do it again? Add your own questions, anything you would like to know.

When you have your material, shape it into a written interview, starting with a few sentences to introduce your subject and then using a simple Q and A format for the body of the article. Finish with a few sentences in conclusion. Take twenty minutes.

If you don't know anyone who has done voluntary work, interview yourself. Ask yourself the same questions about a time you've volunteered and write your introduction and conclusion using the third person for yourself. 'I asked Jenny about the after-school writing club she ran at her local primary school...'

Poetry

There's a wonderful poem by Thomas Lux called 'Ode to the Joyful Ones', celebrating the people who light up our lives with their own delight in living. You can easily find it online. Write a poem celebrating the people who generously give their time to make other people's lives better.

Call it, 'Ode to the Generous Ones.' What do they do? Where do they do it? You could give some examples, either wide-ranging across different kinds of voluntary work or focusing on a particular group or organisation, such as your nearest food bank. Why should we celebrate the people who volunteer?

Put passion into your poem – make it a call to action. Take twenty minutes.

Christmas

Christmas! Love it or hate it, it's everywhere at this time of year – in the shops, on TV and across social media. Families, friends and colleagues are making plans. There will be unexpected joys and disappointments, happy reunions and conflicts, social overload and loneliness, and always nostalgia, all of which makes Christmas a brilliant theme for writing.

If you're really busy in the run-up to Christmas, taking twenty minutes out for a stroll around your inner world with a bit of personal writing is a great way to de-stress and feel re-energised. Or if you have time on your hands, what could be a more pleasurable way to fill it?

So here's a little gift of free-range writing, just for you. Happy Christmas!

> **NOTE:** Not everyone celebrates Christmas, but most cultural traditions have some kind of celebration in December. If don't celebrate Christmas, simply adapt the forays to your own winter celebration.

Memoir

Music is powerfully evocative of the past. Write a list of songs or pieces of music you associate with Christmas, just the first half dozen you think of, from any period in your life.

For example, mine would include the Halleluiah Chorus in St Paul's Cathedral with my father and older sister when we were children and Fairy tale of New York, which was in the mix tape one of my sons made for a family Christmas in the Highlands.

Choose one.

Listen to your piece of music or, if it's very long, a section of it, for up to five minutes. If you don't have it in your collection, you can find it online.

Let the music flow through you. Don't try to focus your ideas, but just notice the passing thoughts, feelings and memories the music brings. Notice the effects of the music in your physical body too.

When the music has finished, let it go. Don't listen again. Your writing will not be about the music itself, but about the memories it has brought back to you.

Write the story of a particular memory, inspired by the music. Take about fifteen minutes.

Fiction

In this story, someone who is hosting some kind of Christmas party or gathering in their home. Who? Write a few notes about them – their name, age and something about their appearance.

Who is at the gathering – lots of people, or just a few? Is the party just beginning, just ending or in full swing? Picture the scene. Jot down some notes.

An unexpected guest arrives. Who?

Is the visitor welcome or unwelcome?

What does the host do?

What happens next?

Write the story. Twenty minutes.

Non-Fiction

The numbered list is a popular form of article in blogs and magazines because it's easy to write and makes a quick read. For this piece, write a list of Christmas gift suggestions for a particular group, choosing a theme you know about, such as 'Five great gifts for quilters/gardeners/ kids age 7-9...'

Begin with a sentence or two of introduction and end with a sentence in conclusion, summing up your theme. Take twenty minutes.

Poetry

Write a list of five objects that are part of your Christmas traditions, either now or in the past – for example, a particular bauble, garment or table decoration. Go with the first ones you think of.

Objects have both objective and subjective layers of

meaning; they are what we all agree they are and also what each of us associates with them personally. For example, I used to have a Father Christmas mug. To everyone else it was just a naff novelty mug, but it had many happy associations for me. Personal meanings carry emotion, as well as information.

Think about one of the objects on your list. Write the first words that come into your head when you look at it. For my mug, those might be, 'Christmas stockings, family, Cornwall.'

What would your object say to you if it could speak? My mug would say, 'Your kids know you so well!'

How does your object feel about being part of your Christmas – friendly, hostile, bored? I think my mug was happy to come out of the cupboard at Christmas, but also quite happy to go back in.

If you were chatting about old times, what stories would your object tell?

Repeat this with the rest of the objects on your list.

Symbolism is the language of poetry, so simply finding symbolic resonances is the task here but, if you'd like to, you could write a poem as well. Write it in the first person, as one of the objects on your list. Try to capture its mood and voice. Enjoy!

YOUR BIRTHDAY BONUS

Happy Birthday!

How do you feel about your birthdays? Some people love them, some people don't; some birthdays might feel more challenging or more exciting than others. However you feel, writing is a brilliant way of taking some you-time when things feel hectic or emotional. So, on your special day, treat yourself to a few delicious writing breaks with some birthday themed free-range writing.

The timings are there to help you not to feel intimidated by the blank page or worry prematurely about writing well. Personal writing and first drafts are not supposed to be good. As Hemingway famously said, the first draft of anything is sh*t. That is a true and liberating thought!

Memoir

How did your family celebrate your birthday when you were a child? Think back as far as you can remember, to your earliest birthday memories, and scan forward through the rest of your childhood. Then carry on into your adult years, right up to the present day. Imagine these memories as snapshot moments. They are likely to be a mixed bag.

Snap! This is me finding my brand new second hand bike propped up in the hall, with a ribbon round the handlebars, age about six.

Snap! Me, age seven or eight, at my first and only birthday party.

Snap! A birthday tea, my boyfriend, my parents, one or two siblings and me. Age about fifteen. Awkward.

My twenty-first, a grassy bank, no family, a broke boyfriend, twenty-one liquorice comfits and a bottle of fizzy wine. My fortieth, picnic in the car with the kids, rain clattering on the roof, a little bit of perfect.

Take a maximum of five minutes for this initial pondering.

Which of these snapshots would you like to put in your birthday album? Choose three. Look more closely at these pictures in your mind. Who else is in them? What is in the background?

Write for five minutes about each one, simply describing what you see. Finish each of these little word sketches off with a title and date.

Fiction

Someone is in a bad mood on their birthday. Who? Make some notes on this character.

What exactly are they feeling – for example, sulky, angry, sad – and why are they feeling this way?

Something happens that breaks the mood. What? It's a birthday story, so we want a happy ending!

Write the story.

Take twenty minutes.

> TIP: Fiction plots always work on two levels, the action and the psychological journey of the protagonist. Either way in will lead you to finding the plot.

Non-Fiction

This task is about the benefits and drawbacks of being your current age. Start straight in and keep going until you can't think of any more benefits and drawbacks.

Begin with 'The good thing about being (your current age) is...'

Start the next sentence, 'But the bad thing about being (your current age) is…'

Reduce the prompts for the second two things, to 'The good thing/ The bad thing', and again for all the subsequent ones, to just 'Good/Bad.'

Keep going for as long as you like, but start and end with a good thing because it's your birthday and focusing on the good stuff is the way to a happy day.

> TIP: Try this exercise as your protagonist if you normally write fiction. Find out how they feel about the benefits and drawbacks of different aspects of their current situation.

Poetry

What would you like for your birthday? Write whatever comes for five minutes. Some fancy bath bombs, a straw sun hat, a hot stones massage, a cure for migraine, world peace…

Do you notice any themes emerging? How do the things you want reflect you as a person, your values and attitudes?

Choosing some of the elements from your prose warm-up, write a birthday list and then make your list into a poem. Think about the voice of the poem – are you going for serious or tongue-in-cheek? Take fifteen minutes.

When you have finished, imagine you have all the things on your list. Close your eyes for a moment. Enjoy. Let this happy imagining be a little birthday gift to yourself.

Happy birthday!

TICK LIST

January		
	Diving In	
	The Wisdom of Pooh	
	New Beginnings	
	World Snow Day	
February		
	Storytelling Week	
	Book Giving	
	Black Monday	
	Random Acts of Kindness	
March		
	Happiness	
	Old Stuff	
	Mother's Day	
	Make Your Day	
April		
	April Fool's Day	
	Earth Day	
	Unicorns	
	Pets	

May		
	Walking	
	Mental Health	
	Dying Matters	
	Biscuits	
June		
	Reading Groups	
	Father's Day	
	Knitting	
	Writing Day	
July		
	Seaside	
	Plastic	
	Staycations	
August		
	Play	
	Owls	
	Afternoon Tea	
	More Holidays!	
	Youth	
September		
	Swap ideas Day	
	World Peace	
	Learning	
	Procrastination	

October		
	World Post Day	
	Older People	
	Libraries	
	Drawing	
November		
	Bonfire Night	
	NaNoWriMo	
	Stress	
	Road Safety	
December		
	Handmade Gifts	
	Elf Day	
	Volunteering	
	Christmas	
Your Birthday Bonus		
	Happy birthday!	

JENNY ALEXANDER'S OTHER BOOKS FOR WRITERS

Writing in the House of Dreams: Unlock the Power of Your Unconscious Mind is all about inspiration – where it comes from and how to keep it coming.

'An astonishing book. I don't think I've read another like it' ~ Susan Price, Carnegie Medal Winner.

Happy Writing: Beat Your Blocks, Be Published and Find Your Flow is about how to keep going with a longer project or through the ups and downs of a long writing career.

'A wonderful book… wise and inspirational' ~ Linda Newbery, Costa Prize Winner.

Free-Range Writing: 75 Forays for the Wild Writer's Soul will help you push your writing limits and build your skills, either on your own or with your writing group.

'Like the author's teaching style – clear, warm and full of sound advice' ~ Jane Moss, Host at The Writing Retreat.

Notes to Self: Tips and Reminders to Help you Keep Writing – bitesize inspirations and observations on writing, with space for you to add your own

To find out more about Jenny Alexander's books and creative courses, visit https://jennyalexander.co.uk/ where you can also sign up for her 'Life, Writing, Workshops' monthly newsletter.

www.ingramcontent.com/pod-product-compliance
Lightning Source LLC
Chambersburg PA
CBHW030300100526
44590CB00012B/456